AWAKENING THE RAINMAKER

AWAKENING THE RAINMAKER

A Guide to Gender Equality

Nishtha Anand

BLOOMSBURY
NEW DELHI • LONDON • OXFORD • NEW YORK • SYDNEY

BLOOMSBURY INDIA
Bloomsbury Publishing India Pvt. Ltd
Second Floor, LSC Building No. 4, DDA Complex, Pocket C – 6 & 7,
Vasant Kunj, New Delhi 110070

BLOOMSBURY, BLOOMSBURY INDIA and the Diana logo
are trademarks of Bloomsbury Publishing Plc

First published in India 2021
This edition published 2021

ISBN: PB: 978-93-54350-61-0; eBook: 978-93-54350-77-1

2 4 6 8 10 9 7 5 3 1

Typeset in Fournier MT Std by Manipal Technologies Limited
Printed and bound in India by Thomson Press India Ltd.

MIX
Paper from responsible sources
FSC® C010615

To find out more about our authors and books visit www.bloomsbury.com and sign up for our newsletters

Dedicated to all mothers.
And, the answer to my prayers,
Ditya—may you grow up in a
world ever progressing north.

At times our own light goes out and is rekindled by a spark from another person. Each of us has cause to think with deep gratitude of those who have lighted the flame within us.

—Albert Schweitzer

Nobel Peace Prize (1952), doctor, missionary, philosopher and musician

CONTENTS

#RainmakerSpeak

ACKNOWLEDGEMENTS

As far as my memory goes, I have always been passionate about gender equality. I wanted to be the best in whatever I pursued and make my parents proud. As a child, I loved to act and dance to '*Papa kehte hain bada kaam [karegi]*'. I cannot pinpoint the exact reason why I had this drive for achievement from such a young age. It is hard to know whether it had something to do with growing up in a predominantly female household—society at large always saw something lacking in our family unit—or if it was the subtle gendered signs one gets while growing up, from relatives, teachers or even strangers, who are always ready with their friendly advice on how girls should talk, walk and behave, to achieve the zenith of marital and maternal success. Thank heavens for my brain's wiring that I took all the unsolicited advice in my stride and focused on doing just the opposite—on achieving academic and professional success. The constant, unwavering support of my parents, sister and husband has helped me stay the way I am—a gender-equality enthusiast who, with this book, is working towards bettering things for women right from the start, the moment they utter that first cry as a baby when they enter this world.

When I was pregnant with my first child, despite reading enough literature on how women can manage their personal and professional lives better and the steps one can take towards perfecting the art of becoming a multitasking diva, I still found myself quite overwhelmed. That is where the genesis of the idea for writing a handbook promoting gender equality came to me. I decided to voraciously read, interview and interact with other women, to bring together the less-talked-about fact that for a woman to continue her career uninterrupted, in addition to her own efforts, she needs support from her family—spouse, parents, in-laws—and policy support from her organisation. This book is an attempt to help women realise that they should question their lives when they are expected to choose between their family and their career. A woman's life can also shape up like that of her father, brother or husband, where she too can simultaneously have a professional and personal life. To achieve this, she needs to stop living the myth that women can do it all and needs to start unapologetically delegating household responsibilities to free up the much-needed bandwidth to pursue her passion.

In the process of writing the book, besides extensive secondary research, I also interviewed and interacted with some phenomenal women who have beautifully managed their personal and professional lives and are now embodying their gender-inclusion vision at their respective organisations. I would like to extend my heartfelt gratitude to all these ladies who spared time for a first-time author (in alphabetical order): Chhavi Mittal, Kalpana Morparia, Lizzie Chapman, Meher Pudumjee, Naiyya Saggi, Raspreet Sidhu, Reeba Chacko, Renu Sud Karnad, Dr Rohini Godbole

(Padma Shri), Sonia Gupta, Dr Sujatha Ramdorai, Sukhleen Aneja and Zia Mody.

I would also like to thank some more ladies who feel passionately about the subject and shared their experiences and domain knowledge on the matter: Devjani Sharma, Japleen Pasricha and Payal Gupta.

Thanks to Sarbani Mukherjea, who was there all along the way as a sounding board and trusted advisor whose editing inputs I valued greatly.

A shout-out to my dear friends, who were helpful in varied ways and means through my writing journey: Jasmeet Kaur Grover, Shagun Gupta, Prerna Parija, Gunjan Karthik, Sonam Jain and Ganesh Iyer.

Last but not least, a few lines for my husband, Narendra Rathi, for being a true partner and standing behind me as I pursued my passion project. He relentlessly spent many sleepless nights brainstorming with me so that this book offers the best to all its readers. Just like behind every successful man there is a woman, a woman too needs her man beside her to succeed in her pursuits.

WHY THIS BOOK?

A rainmaker is someone who, through their wide network and influence, brings in monetary success and increased brand value for a business. With their connections, contacts and clout, they are integral to the success of any company, especially in terms of generating revenue. Given their immense contribution to the top line, rainmakers are put on a pedestal in any organisation and enjoy massive power and authority. They often have the last word on important decisions and matters such as employee bonuses, promotions, hiring and dismissals. They project confidence, as they know how important their contributions are, and seldom mince words, being articulate in their opinions.

The word 'rainmaker' was added to my vocabulary after my MBA when I started my career in investment banking. These rainmakers were role models to youngsters who, like me, were at the threshold of a corporate career. It didn't take me long to notice that these superstars were always men. Not once did I come across a woman in such a powerful role. I switched two organisations after my first job, but the situation was the same everywhere. However, what I did come across were the struggles of several women in the workforce, a majority of whom worked in operational or support roles or were stuck in junior and mid-level positions.

A lot of these women were not assertive enough for mainstream revenue roles, and those who had made it to more powerful positions were in a constant struggle trying to prove themselves worthy.

This absence of female rainmakers bothered me. Could I ever become one for my organisation? I was not sure.

The curious case of the missing XX chromosome!

As I dived deep into this aspect of the Indian corporate world, a few things stood out to me:

- The limited participation of women in the workforce: the economic contribution of Indian women is 17 per cent of the GDP, which is less than half the global average (compared with 40 per cent in China).[1]
- Leadership roles are dominated by men: only 12 per cent of women make it to the C-suite[2], and just 20 per cent of businesses in India are run by women, of which 79 per cent are self-funded[3] (most women entrepreneurs struggle to raise funding from venture capitalists).

[1] https://www.worldbank.org/en/news/speech/2018/03/17/women-indias-economic-growth

[2] https://economictimes.indiatimes.com/magazines/panache/india-inc-sees-early-gender-gaps-with-34-drop-in-women-frontline-leaders-only-12-make-it-to-c-suite/articleshow/72884002.cms?from=mdr

[3] https://in.makers.yahoo.com/one-woman-army-meet-the-solo-woman-entrepreneurs-who-raised-the-largest-funding-amount-in-india-055043302.html

- Several women drop out mid-way in their career: 20 million Indian women dropped out of the workforce between 2005 to 2012. This is equivalent to the entire population of Sri Lanka.[4]

In an attempt to unravel the mystery behind the lack of women rainmakers, I connected with and read about several successful men and women who shared their professional experiences and life stories with me. In the process, I was fascinated to discover how different an Indian woman's life cycle is, compared to her male counterpart's.

The difference between the upbringing of boys and girls starts in early childhood when most young girls are subconsciously primed for domesticity. As they grow up, this gap widens further for those girls who start adopting a submissive demeanour, leading them to make career choices from a disadvantaged position, as they are always torn between their family and career. As an olive to this cocktail comes the infamous glass ceiling in the corporate world, adding to the challenges of every working woman. To bridge the gap between a man's and a woman's career trajectory, a concerted effort by the woman's parents, spouses, in-laws, peers, corporates and, most importantly, by the women themselves is necessary. This book tries to capture some of these problems through various case studies and draws upon diverse experiences to find solutions to achieve gender parity.

[4] https://www.worldbank.org/en/news/speech/2018/03/17/women-indias-economic-growth

The graph below summarises how social norms influence men and women differently:

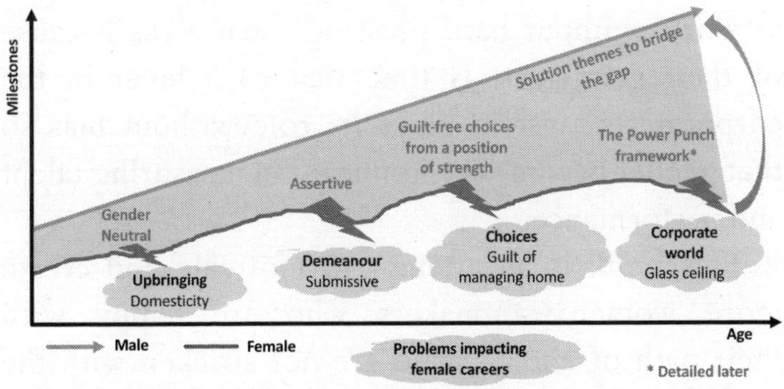

While all women need societal support, the corporate woman needs additional assistance in terms of organisational policies and behaviour. This is important, given the absence of a level playing field for men and women. Talent is the backbone of any organisation, and attracting the best talent is impossible if the working environment is not conducive for 50 per cent of the talent pool. Long strides are being made by several organisations in achieving gender equality and inclusion in the true sense, and I have made an effort to laud the good work done by such companies. In places where I have identified some gaps, I have suggested guidelines that can go a long way in achieving gender inclusion. I have also defined a framework called 'The Power Punch', which describes what an organisation, and the different influencers within an organisation, should do to ensure a gender-agnostic ecosystem. We have had many books addressing what women need to do to be able to manage a career and a household. In this book, in addition to covering similar themes,

I have also focused on what women can expect from the organisations to which they commit their diligence and intellect, to be able to give their best at work, without hard-pressing themselves because of their gender. It is time that each lever in the corporate ecosystem plays its role without bias so that gender becomes insignificant in measuring talent and performance.

This book is an attempt to motivate and create more women rainmakers who are happy with their path of choice, who are not stricken with the guilt of either missing out on family life or for not pursuing their dreams and ambitions. So, go ahead and enjoy the read! If you find the ideas in the book resonating with you, please embody them. Let's awaken the rainmaker in us and in those around us! *#BeaRainmaker*

In the process of writing the book, I interacted with and interviewed several women from different fields: established corporate leaders, thought leaders, entrepreneurs and sports personalities. These interactions have been incorporated in the book as *#RainmakerSpeak*. They throw light on the journeys of these phenomenal women, right from their upbringing, their outlook on life, the choices they have made, their approach to gender equality and how they are implementing it in their organisations and embodying it in their lives. As you read through their stories, you will realise that each one has had her own mountain to conquer, and yet, they have all continued to move ahead, balancing their personal life and pursuing their passion with determination and self-will. There were some common themes that came across in all these interactions:

- Gender-neutral upbringing
- An assertive demeanour
- A marriage of equals—a supportive spouse goes a long way in enabling a woman's career
- Good time management to prioritise what is important and what is not

Most of us face similar dilemmas and stand at similar crossroads when choosing our paths. In these moments, I hope the advice from this book and the learnings from *#RainmakerSpeak* come in handy for all my readers.

To achieve gender equality in the corporate world, the conduct of women themselves and the organisation's stance on the matters of gender equality go hand in hand. My conversations with professionals from human resources (HR) teams of several organisations made it evident that many are doing great work in the pursuit of equal opportunities. Based on my extensive research, I have defined some *#PowerPolicies* that I recommend as a guide to all professionals across all levels of management. Only when we acknowledge and learn from the best in the industry—for whom equality is not just a social agenda but rather a business strategy to ensure elevated financial performance, higher brand value and thriving business culture—will gender equality be pursued by all companies seriously rather than perfunctorily.

I hope that the work presented in this book acts as a handbook for everyone—from employees (so they know what they can expect as part of a respectful and inclusive work environment) to decision-makers (so they are abreast with the strides made by other organisations)—so that they eventually make a roadmap for their respective organisations to stand tall on gender equality and inclusion.

#RainmakerSpeak

Meher Pudumjee, chairperson, Thermax Limited

I have always been an ardent fan of strong women, even as a child. The memory of dressing up as Rani Lakshmi Bai, the unforgettable lines from the renowned poem by Subhadra Kumari Chauhan that pays tribute to the warrior queen's bravery, '*Khoob ladi mardaani woh toh Jhansi wali rani thi…*', are still fresh in my mind. I now understand how listening to stories about strong, independent women shaped who I am today. With this thought in mind, let's meet this exemplary lady, a rainmaker who beautifully balances her professional and personal life. I hope that her story inspires everyone reading this, especially women, and motivates them to pursue their passion.

At a young age, she along with her husband took over the responsibility of turning around the loss-making foreign subsidiary of her family-owned company. The challenges she and her husband faced while successfully turning the business around, how she managed motherhood during this time and her approach to balancing her family and her career are all commendable. After talking to her, I realised how a gender-agnostic upbringing laid a strong foundation during her formative years. This led her to becoming a strong, assertive woman, someone who could make her own choices and pursue her passions. Meher Pudumjee, one who always had a plan and executed it beautifully, says, 'Play to express, rather than impress.'

Meher is a chemical engineer by qualification and the chairperson of Thermax Ltd, one of India's leading engineering companies in the energy, environment and chemical domain. Thermax has a global presence spread over 29 countries and 14 state-of-the-art manufacturing facilities across India, Indonesia, Denmark and Poland. Meher is counted amongst the 50 most powerful women in India by *Fortune India* in its 'India's 50 most Powerful Women in Business' list. She represented India at the Asian Business Women's Conference in Osaka in 2006. Two years later, the World Economic Forum selected her as a Young Global Leader. In 2009, *Business Standard* named her CEO of the Year. A mother of two, Meher is a philanthropist, musician and board member of not-for-profit organisations such as Teach for India and Shakti Sustainable Energy Foundation. She chairs the board of the Akanksha Foundation and is a member of Social Venture Partners in the city of Pune.

Foundation stone: Gender-neutral upbringing

Meher had a gender-neutral upbringing. Her parents believed in giving the best education to her brother Kurush and her. Meher was good at maths and science and therefore decided to study engineering. Encouraged by her parents, she pursued a four-year postgraduate degree in chemical engineering from Imperial College of Science, Technology and Medicine, London. This was unlike the upbringing her mother, Anu Aga, had in her childhood, where she was prepared for domesticity. But destiny had a different plan and Anu had to take the reins of Thermax when her husband, Rohinton Aga, suddenly passed away in 1996. With her own life experiences, Anu realised that most women start with a script that is not helpful for pursuing a career. But we cannot blame our past and must take action. This action-oriented approach led Anu to professional achievement as she successfully fulfilled the role of the chairperson of Thermax from 1996 to 2004, and under her leadership, Thermax not only turned its business around but also strengthened its position and grew in profits.

Anu and her husband knew the pivotal role a gender-neutral education plays while raising children. Therefore, they brought up their children differently, giving them the space and freedom to choose what they wanted to be. While Anu did not have any women role models from the world of business, Meher had a mentor in her mother.

Talking about the early days in the business, Meher explained, 'I was extremely nervous when I was taking over Thermax as chairperson after my mother because I had so much to live up to. At that time, she advised me, "Remember, an apple tree can't give oranges. You are you, be yourself, don't try to ape your parents, do what you think is right since you have so much to offer." That helped me gain a lot of confidence. I realised that I have to be comfortable being myself. But more than the advice, just how she has lived her life is an inspiration for me, and that to me is far more important than any advice.'

Choices: Running parallel tracks

Meher has had a very successful career all along, right from the time she joined Thermax as an engineering trainee in 1990. A year later, she moved to the UK along with her husband Pheroz to manage and turn around a loss-making company. The five years they spent there were of great learning for both Meher and Pheroz. They were managing a cash-strapped company in a foreign land, and they had to work from scratch on everything: turn-around strategies, negotiating with suppliers and lenders, and conceptualising new product lines that could cater better to the foreign clientele. Meher and Pheroz always acknowledge the role of Dr Joshi, their mentor and guide, who spent the first year with them in the UK, along with another engineer, Ravi Chidambaram. During this time, Meher had her first child. The first thought that usually crops up in a woman's mind on becoming a mother is to give up her career and channel every bit of her being into taking care of the child. Even if she doesn't want to do this willingly, the family encourages women to make such a choice. Luckily for Meher, her mother Anu helped her with childcare for the first six months after she had her baby. Motherhood presented Meher with an opportunity to grow, to be someone her children could look up to, both personally and professionally. Instead of giving up her career, Meher focused on prioritising her time in a way that she could be a parent as well as a woman who continued to pursue her passion. Meher said, 'Time management was the biggest lesson I learnt during my time in the UK. Both Pheroz and I used to work for more than twelve hours a day. Then, I had my son three years into living in the UK, and at six months of age, I would have to pick him up from the babysitter at three in the afternoon each day. My first thought was, how will I manage to finish so much work in that time? But, you won't believe that just by prioritising and defining what was important and what was less important, I got as much, if not more, covered from 9 AM to 3 PM.'

Since I was facing the same dilemma, being a first-time mother, I asked Meher about the balancing act between motherhood and a career, and what her advice would be to women on tackling motherhood guilt, since every woman faces this at some point or the other.

'I would say that I was a better mother since I was a working professional, and it went a long way in shaping up my children's personalities. They became quite independent, self-reliant and confident. As they were growing up, I made a rule to not sweat about the small things. Instead, I defined a broad parameter for my kids, with dos and don'ts about very few but important things. I also made a point of being there for my kids at every important milestone, big or small. I was with them at their parent-teacher meetings, at basketball matches and school concerts. I ensured that every minute that I spent with my kids was happy, and for that, I had to stop micromanaging. For instance, when it came to their homework, since I usually ended up losing my patience when I got down to it with them, I ensured that they would go for tuitions or did it on their own. Thus, I always strived for a cheerful relationship with my kids, where they could feel comfortable coming to me for any help or guidance. I definitely think being a working mother helped me achieve this.

'But there were moments when I would feel guilty for missing out on things because I was working. In those moments, I would remind myself that my work makes me happy and as a happy woman I make a better mother! In my view, all women, if they have a passion, they should pursue it, whether it is in the for-profit or the social sector. It makes you feel wholesome to be able to learn and value-add and also spend time with your loved ones. It's important to find a balance, make your own support system—delegate shamelessly, rely on your joint family or house help, so you can give your passion a chance,' explained Meher practically.

Corporate leadership and beyond

By design, the engineering and manufacturing industry is one that sees fewer women than men. Nevertheless, Meher attempts to make Thermax a place where female talent is attracted and encouraged to make a career if they so choose. Here is what she had to say about this.

'If you ask women employees at Thermax whether they enjoy working here, if they feel safe in the organisation, whether they feel challenged, the answers would be a resounding yes! Having said that, our numbers are still dismally low, with less than

7 per cent of our staff being women. We have tried a few initiatives over the past few years to try and raise the numbers. To begin with, we have given the mandate to recruit at least 20 per cent women at the graduate engineer trainee level. At the internship level, we have tried to take in more women interns during their summer breaks or during their third-year engineering projects, also between 20 to 25 per cent. Women don't often have professional role models, so our HR team started a forum at Thermax called "Sakhi", where we invite women leaders from other businesses to come and talk about their professional journey, their key learnings, successes and challenges. We have an interesting programme termed 'Second Innings' where women are given an opportunity to resume their professional journey after a sabbatical through a flexible five-hour-a-day work arrangement for a six-month period to start with.

'We also have interns speaking about what it is like to be a woman working at Thermax. Unfortunately, not many women like to join a manufacturing, engineering workplace. Most want to join the IT sector. My mother and I sometimes address them and listen to their issues. We make an effort to help them be more assertive, even if it ever came to sexual harassment. The company also started sensitising men about how to look at the Prevention of Sexual Harassment (POSH) Act. Working from home is something we were keen to try two years ago, as this may have been attractive for women, but there was a lot of resistance since the management was afraid of losing productivity, effectiveness, etc.

I also feel that within any organisation, giving too many favours to any one gender is not a healthy approach. Despite all these measures, we still have a lot more to do, to increase the numbers.'

My interaction with Meher gave me an insight into the amazing career she has had while overcoming her share of challenges. Her success has been driven by her commitment to pursuing her passion while making practical choices when it came to time management and delegating an appropriate amount of work so she could balance her professional and personal life. Today she is a happy mother and an accomplished professional.

Meher's journey brings to the fore the crucial role of upbringing. A gender-neutral childhood is the first stepping stone towards the road of equality. And it is imperative for parents to be aware of the subtle and not-so-subtle messages they give their children and thus perpetuate gender biases. If we are made to believe in our potential in our formative years, we are the lucky ones who can achieve whatever we set our eyes on. This belief translates into confidence in dealing with situations and making life choices from a position of strength, free from the clutches of gender-related self-doubt that holds us back. With this in mind, let's dive into the first section of the book, which covers the stepping stones to nurturing young girls into becoming strong and confident women who feel free to pursue their passions and live fuller personal and professional lives.

Section I:

UPBRINGING, DEMEANOUR AND THE UNDERLYING CHOICE TO BE HAPPY

I

First Hurdle: Chinks in Upbringing

Children must be taught how to think, not what to think.

—Margaret Mead

Cultural anthropologist and writer

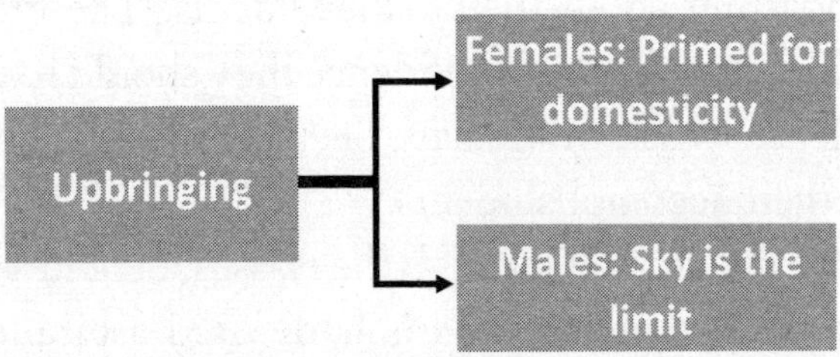

During my formative years, the world seemed perfect. There seemed to be no dichotomy in the environment around me. My parents enrolled me in nursery school, and there were broadly the same number of girls and boys in the class. We learnt the same things, took part in the same activities and were given the same opportunities. However, as I progressed through the school years, I sensed a shift somewhere around middle school. The difference gradually became quite evident in the mannerisms of the male and the female students.

The boys were more aggressive—they seemed more confident than the girls. They didn't care much when they made mistakes or when they disappointed the teacher in any way. Their attitude towards the girls in the class also altered. Something had given them the innate confidence that they were better than the girls in anything physical, analytical and advanced, and therefore sports, maths and science were their domains. The seed of bias had already taken root in their minds and was at play. Meanwhile, the girls continued to work diligently, with an attitude of compliance and obedience. They continued to score better than the boys in all the subjects, including maths and science, yet they were not seen boasting about their achievements. The girls did not project the kind of confidence they should have, the confidence which would have been completely justified, given their accomplishments.

As we progressed through the classes, I could see that only a small number of girls harboured aspirations to make it big in the world by contributing to the fields of medicine, physics, business, economics, etc. Somewhere along the way, the majority had taken a turn for a different road that focused on completing basic studies, becoming a graduate, marrying well and raising a family. If there was any glimmer of ambition, it was directed towards professions that are perceived as being more home-friendly, with more regulated hours, such as the role of a school teacher, a bank employee or a less demanding government job. Although each of these professions requires hard work and dedication, the broad perception is that these professions allow a working woman to strike a balance along with managing a family.

If we were still being taught the same subjects by the same teachers, then what was causing this change? Why was half of India's talent not focused on realising its full potential?

Women start quite well as children. They are hard-working high achievers, competing on a level playing field with the boys. But as they grow older, their upbringing and social conditioning change their aspirations and dreams, in terms of what they need to achieve. There are two key pillars within a successful family structure—managing a household and bringing the family together have traditionally been a woman's domain, while earning money and managing finances have primarily been a man's job. This division of work has evolved through time and civilisations (though I strongly argue that this evolution is still a work in progress!). There are limited examples of all-rounders, male and female, managing both aspects of work single-handedly and successfully. Thus, the mantra for a well-rounded life that children have learnt over generations and which they also learn by observing us is that the endgame for women is producing children and taking care of the family, leaving the outside world for men to handle.

Today, there is an increasing perception that women can be career-oriented, looking beyond the realm of household work. However, despite their capabilities, society continues to suggest that the safe avenue for women is to go for less strenuous and consequently lower-paying careers because the primary responsibility for the household and the raising of children still lies with the woman.

The emotional play by our parents and years of social conditioning make us believe that we are more suited to take care of the home and family, and if required, work in stable environments. We are made to accept that our natural talents and desire for happiness lie in focusing on domestic life. The ones who manage to take a stand of going against these accepted norms are made to feel guilty for ignoring their family and, above all, their children. Due to such conditioning of women from an early age, the world has been missing out on potential contributions towards growth and development by half the workforce.

While researching this subject, I came to read about Warren Buffett's views on the issue. Buffett mentioned how in their younger years, his sisters (Buffett has two sisters)—smart and capable girls—were advised to marry early and well, while he was taught that the sky was the limit for him.

> [My] possibilities dwarfed those of my siblings, for I was a boy! [...] at every turn my sisters would be told—more through signals than words—that success for them would be 'marrying well.' I was meanwhile hearing that the world's opportunities were there for me to seize...[1]

While parents have the best interests of their children at heart, they inadvertently end up advocating beliefs based on their own experiences or on the ideas they believe in. The inherent assumption that household

[1] Buffett, W. 2013. 'Warren Buffett is Bullish ... On Women'. *Fortune*, 2 May. Available at: *https://fortune.com/2013/05/02/warren-buffett-is-bullish-on-women/*

work is a woman's responsibility and the fact that most mothers take care of their family members as a full-time job make them feel it is onerous for women to take on careers.

As I reflected on how crucial a role upbringing plays in shaping the trajectory of our lives and influencing the choices we make in the future, I came across the work of Margaret Mead (1901–1978), an American cultural anthropologist and writer, famous for her work and publications on societal issues. Her ground-breaking work on culture and childrearing continues to be of prominence today. She was inducted into the National Women's Hall of Fame in 1976 and was posthumously awarded the Presidential Medal of Freedom in 1979. As I read Mead's work, I could see that the reality of today's world is aligned with her famous theory of imprinting, which states that children learn by observing adult behaviour.

Mead argued that personality characteristics, especially the difference between men and women, are shaped by cultural conditioning rather than heredity.[2] 'I had no reason to doubt that brains were suitable for a woman. And as I had my father's kind of mind—which was also his mother's—I learned that the mind is not sex-typed.'[3]

She emphasised the importance of society looking beyond traditional gender stereotypes while also being vocal about how motherhood and career can go hand in hand. She said, 'There is no evidence that suggests women are naturally better at caring for children ...

[2] https://www.biography.com/scholar/margaret-mead

[3] Lewis, J.J. 2020. 'Margaret Mead Quotes'. *ThoughtCo*, 26 August. Available at: thoughtco.com/margaret-mead-quotes-3525400

with the fact of child-bearing out of the center of attention, there is even more reason for treating girls first as human beings, then as women.'[4]

Similar concerns came to the fore during several of my interactions with women in different fields, who are professionally well-placed, yet, influenced by their childhood conditioning, continue to get encircled by self-doubt. Therefore, it came as no surprise to me that a KPMG 2019 study[5] concluded that only 22 per cent of professional women felt that their parents instilled in them the value of self-confidence. The more commonly taught values to them were hard work (66 per cent) and respect (57 per cent). There's no denying that hard work and respect serve every professional well in their career, but if one aspires for senior and leadership roles, then self-confidence is one of the key traits required. Therefore, childhood conditioning is an essential reason why many women shy away from taking bigger risks in furthering their careers, thereby missing out on a number of opportunities. This lack of self-confidence also manifests itself as the 'imposter syndrome', where women question their talents and abilities. This self-doubt can make a woman feel that she's not prepared for the promotion she is being offered or that she's not equipped to lead the new high-stakes project she has been asked to head. This acts as a deterrent for them on a number of counts—they are less confident in

[4] Lewis, J.J. 2020. 'Margaret Mead Quotes'. *ThoughtCo*, 26 August. Available at: thoughtco.com/margaret-mead-quotes-3525400

[5] '2019 KPMG Women's Leadership Study' (https://info.kpmg.us/content/dam/info/en/news-perspectives/pdf/2019/KPMG_Womens_Leadership_Study.pdf); Copyright (c) 2019 KPMG LLP. All rights reserved. Sourced with permission.

highlighting their achievements, taking initiatives for big projects, negotiating for a better salary and moving cities for a job.[6]

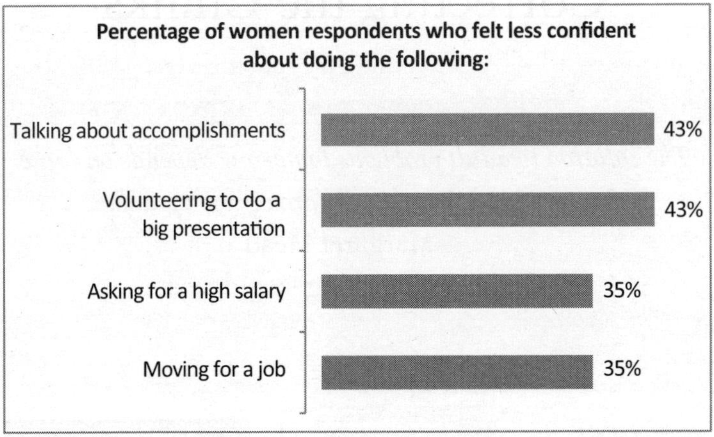

Percentage of women respondents who felt less confident about doing the following:

To strive for a truly equal world where growth is driven by both genders, these chinks in upbringing need to be addressed. Since we reap what we sow, unless we sow the principle of equality in our future generations now, we will continue with our struggle with reaping the benefits of gender parity. According to the Global Gender Gap Report 2021 by the World Economic Forum, it will take 135.6 years to close the gender gap worldwide.[7] If this is not a call for action to all adults and parents, I don't know what is!

[6] '2019 KPMG Women's Leadership Study' (https://info.kpmg.us/content/dam/info/en/news-perspectives/pdf/2019/KPMG_Womens_Leadership_Study.pdf); Copyright (c) 2019 KPMG LLP. All rights reserved. Sourced with permission.

[7] 'Global Gender Gap Report 2021' (http://www3.weforum.org/docs/WEF_GGGR_2021.pdf); Copyright (c) 2021 World Economic Forum. All rights reserved.

2

Correcting the Chinks

The solution to adult problems tomorrow depends on large measure upon how our children grow up today.

—Margaret Mead

Cultural anthropologist and writer

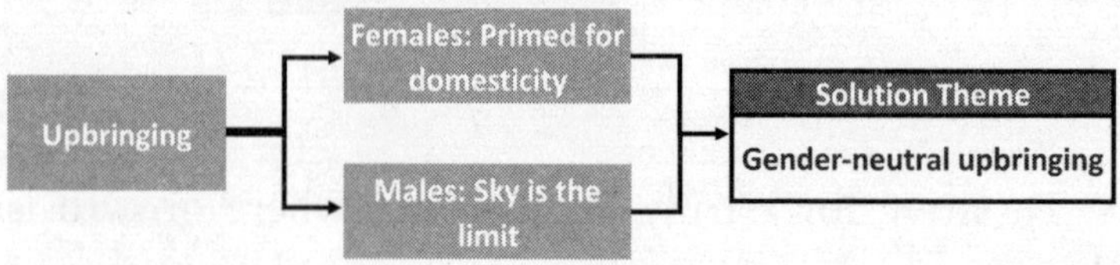

Until a few decades ago, the roles of men and women were compartmentalised—men were the sole breadwinners for the family and were the ones stepping out in the world and bringing in the money; women were responsible for raising the family and managing the house. With the progress made in society, the best thing to happen to women has been the freedom of choice. We can now choose to be what we want:

- a full-time homemaker, managing the house and family,
- a professional woman who manages her household along with her job,
- devote one's life solely to one's career.

In theory, this seems like an easy choice to make, with the decision-making powers lying entirely with the woman, but the reality is far from it. How freely we get to make this choice, unrestricted, unhampered by emotional considerations foisted on us by our family—parents, in-laws, partners, children—is still questionable.

For a woman to be able to make this choice objectively, the first enabling factor that comes to my mind is the way she has been brought up. This is where the nostrum of gender-neutral upbringing comes in. But what is new in this? We are all familiar with this concept, and coming from modern Indian families, we are definitely implementing it. But is that really happening?

Take a deep breath, close your eyes and run through all the interactions you have had with your children. Who do you ask to help in the kitchen more often, encourage to learn to do the laundry, dictate what to wear and what not to wear, ask to sit in a certain way, talk in a certain way? Do you, or your family members, believe that your daughter should learn how to cook, be homely and pleasant, shouldn't be as aggressive and outspoken as her brother? That her grades, while being good, don't have to be brilliant for a prospective career? If the answer here is a resounding 'No!', then you're doing a great job as a parent, but if there are even a few instances where gender comes to the fore while interacting with your kids, you're not really practising gender neutrality.

A common belief is that the male and female brains are different, and men are more competent in some fields because male brains are bigger than female brains. Scientifically though, there's been no conclusive evidence to support the theory that the size of the female brain affects its functioning in any way.[1] How is it then that men and women have careers that follow vastly different trajectories? Why are women labelled as diligent, compassionate and empathetic, while men are seen as brilliant geniuses with powers of strong logical reasoning and drive to action? It doesn't just stop there; these gendered adjectives are justified citing neuroscientific research that says there is a difference in the way a man and woman's brain is wired. Sadly, till some time back, I too believed this. My belief was at times reaffirmed in the corporate world, where I heard comments about how women think emotionally, are more detail-oriented and are therefore more suited for support functions like HR, legal and operations, while men are better with numbers, apply logic, are action-oriented and thus more suitable for leadership roles. The same logic applies to the field of STEM (science, technology, engineering and mathematics), which is wrongly masculinised, with girls being made to believe from a very young age that their strength lies in pursuing softer disciplines.

Of course, there is no denying the physical difference between a man's and a woman's anatomy, but in matters of the brain, both genders are equal. In fact, there is weak scientific evidence of gender-driven brain differences in newborns.[2] It thus boils down to social conditioning, which prepares boys to be outgoing leaders while girls are primed to become docile caregivers. While we may

[1] Rippon, G. 2019. *The Gendered Brain: The New Neuroscience that Shatters the Myth of the Female Brain*. UK: The Bodley Head.

[2] Ibid.

offer the same education to our sons and daughters, are we really focusing on the same aspects, personality traits and priorities while raising them?

Parents often subconsciously pass on traits like submissiveness, guilt and a sense of responsibility for the whole household to their daughters, while to the sons they pass on assertiveness, ambition and an attitude to express themselves without any inhibitions. This theory became evident in my chat with a dear friend, Prerna Parija, head, enterprise business, at Zomato, who was previously heading one of the largest sales teams of over 300 employees as Zomato's regional business head, North India. She recalled a personal brand image exercise she had done with her team, 'I asked my team members to describe me in three words (the first three adjectives that come to their mind). Most male team members described me as hardworking, honest and positive, while female team members described me as bold or courageous, assertive and smart. I identify myself most with being bold and courageous. I found it interesting that men couldn't see me as courageous or assertive while women working under the same conditions observed it about me. Most of these perceptions are deep-seated and have been formed over the years while growing up. People have always associated men with roles of power and money and women with those of nurture and care. This starts from childhood when we observe our mothers and aunts playing the role of the more caring individual, someone who sacrifices, puts the family before herself. This gets reinforced during adulthood when girls are expected to dress, talk and behave in a certain way and be more compliant with norms of society rather than defining their own rules. Hence, the fix has to start right from childhood, within the family. When a child sees that their father does the cooking or cleaning or childcare with equal responsibility, without getting any special mention, perceptions about social roles would become less gendered.'

Multinational giant Procter & Gamble (P&G) has done its share in a bid to bring about a change in social perceptions through its mainstream advertising. In India, an advertisement campaign run by their detergent brand Ariel struck a chord with me. Under the campaign, Share the Load, the brand came out with a series of television adverts addressing the issue of gender inequality. It shows that even today, doing the laundry is expected to be a woman's task. She may be as qualified as a man and earning at par with him or maybe even more than him, yet it does not put a dent in the age-old ideology of household chores being the primary and sole responsibility of a woman. A particular advert from the series resonates well with the issue we are discussing here.

A mother, while on a call with her daughter, is shown serving food and then cleaning the room of her young son. Her daughter mentions that despite her recent promotion, she is leaving her job because of the overwhelming amount of housework she has to do. The mother seems worried and asks her daughter to reconsider her decision—after all, she will be giving up all the hard work she has done so far. She also asks her daughter to take help from her husband and split the responsibilities. To this, her daughter mentions that her husband doesn't know any housework; hence he is of no help. The mother sounds miffed and wonders how this is possible! She then looks around her son's room and realises where the fault lies. She realises that she too has never taught her son to be a holistic individual and has instead raised him as an entitled prince. The mother then decides to take a small first step by teaching her son how to do the laundry.

The campaign *#ShareTheLoad* was a great success and went viral in numerous countries.

Another brilliant advert by P&G for the Olay product line was *#MakeSpaceForWomen*. It features astronaut Nicole Scott, with TV stars Lilly Singh and Busy Philipps. This is what Nicole had to say about her experience:

> I know what it's like to be one of only a handful of women in a room — or on a space station. It's important for everyone to know that the spaceship doesn't care if you're a boy or girl. That's why I'm thrilled Olay has launched their mission in space to encourage more young women to be fearless in pursuit of a career (in science, technology, engineering or mathematics).[3]

#RainmakerSpeak

Dr Sujatha Ramdorai, Indian mathematician

As a dose of inspiration to young girls who seek to pursue a career in STEM, let me share the conversation I had

[3] https://www.bizjournals.com/cincinnati/news/2020/01/15/p-g-casts-astronaut-other-fearless-women-in-super.html

with Dr Sujatha Ramdorai, an Indian mathematician (algebraic number theorist) known for her work on Iwasawa theory. Dr Sujatha's work has implications in the fields of complex geometry, topology, number theory and cryptography. In recognition of this, she was awarded the ICTP Ramanujan Prize by the International Centre for Theoretical Physics in Italy—she was the first Indian and is the only Indian woman to have won this prestigious award till date.[4] In addition, Dr Sujatha has won several recognitions for her work. She was a member of the National Knowledge Commission and was also the member of the scientific advisory council to the prime minister of India.[5]

Choosing mathematics: A not-so-obvious career choice

I asked Dr Sujatha to share her thoughts on what made her choose mathematics. She highlighted the importance of upbringing and parental support, which led to her choosing the career of her choice.

In her words, 'I cannot stress more on the importance of a nurturing and a supportive environment while growing up. My parents paid equal attention to the education of both me and my brother. I always enjoyed maths and science as a child. When I decided to pursue pure science rather than engineering in my higher studies, I was encouraged to do so by my parents. Back then, our relatives and my father's colleagues

[4] As of 25 March 2021 (https://www.ictp.it/about-ictp/prizes-awards/the-ramanujan-prize/the-ramanujan-prize-winners.aspx).

[5] http://nobelprizeseries.in/tbis/s-ramdorai

disapproved of my choice but my father always maintained that I should do what I enjoy the most. I always loved mathematics but couldn't have pursued it without the encouragement and support provided by my family.'

Compassion and pragmatism go a long way

The other key question I wanted Dr Sujatha's view on was if she faced or observed any gender biases in the field of STEM.

Dr Sujatha very candidly shared her views and experiences. 'Luckily, I had all women teachers for maths throughout my schooling. So, I didn't face any biases. But as I started teaching in universities, some of my female students would come up to me and say that they feel more comfortable voicing their doubts with me compared to the male professors. Given the lack of women in STEM, such instances are not uncommon. I genuinely feel that if there were more women to look up to in the field of STEM, it would give young girls more courage to pursue it as a career.

'Let me share an incident here. I was teaching a course at the Beijing University and a PhD candidate requested to meet me. During our meeting, she started discussing her concerns about managing her responsibility as a mother while continuing her PhD. She shared her struggles on how she had a one-year-old daughter who was living away with her grandparents and she felt guilty about this. She wanted the reassurance from me that she was doing the right thing by continuing her studies. Was the sacrifice worth it? She mentioned that she could only discuss this with me since I was the only woman professor and was a mother who may have stood at similar crossroads in the past. I comforted her and told her she was doing the right thing by pursuing her passion. She had to trust her instincts and her decision of leaving her daughter with her loving and caring grandparents. Also, this was a temporary arrangement but it would enable her to be an inspiration for her own daughter who wouldn't be afraid to pursue her dreams at any age. On such days, I feel great that I could provide motivation to a fellow woman so she continues on her path.

'This also reminded me of my younger days when I was pursuing my PhD. I used to travel for two hours from Andheri to Colaba to attend my lectures, leaving behind my daughter with her grandparents. I can recall that there were some days when my in-laws would be out of town and I would have some important lectures to attend. So, I would bring my daughter to campus with me. In such situations, what helps best is considerate professors and peers. My peers would offer to look after her while I attended my lectures or if that couldn't be managed, some considerate professors would step in and offer help.'

Men can also be compassionate and value equality

We moved on to the next topic—even today, men are the majority in the field. Do they care? I requested Dr Sujatha to share some examples. She explained that men have different points of view, but some do care and they could be role models for other men.

'I had one professor, Mr Sridharan, who was very pragmatic and supportive of women. He genuinely believed that given the right opportunities and support, women can do well in the field of their choice despite the multiple roles they have to play. Most importantly, he was vocal about his views on gender inclusion and it gave a sense of validation to women who were pursuing a career while parallelly managing a family. For instance, he would offer to look after my daughter. Not only this, if any student was unable to attend his lecture because of a genuine reason like the baby being unwell, he would offer to deliver the lecture again. You know policies take time, but such acts of kindness and understanding are very important.

'We have quite a few people who question a woman's ability to be a scientist and to perform well in labs. They use stereotypes like women being more emotional and unable to take criticism well. I have heard some people say that women are a distraction to them and hence should not be encouraged. These thoughts act as obstacles to the success of women in the field. So, I genuinely feel that people like Professor Sridharan need to be more well-known so that more men can support in the ways that he did. Even today, men remain the majority, and sensitisation towards diversity is the need of the hour to ensure that people are more thoughtful and accepting of women in the field of science.'

Words of wisdom

In her concluding thoughts, Dr Sujatha said, 'Teaching compassion starts at home—it is a virtue to be taught to both our sons and daughters; only then will we have a generation of men and women who are truly equal and respectful of one another.'

Based on all the research I did and the interactions I had, I can say that the only way to remove the flaws from our upbringing is to have an unbiased mindset while raising the future generation so that they grow up to be equal in the true sense. I strongly urge mothers and fathers to relook at their parenting styles and go beyond the traditional gender-driven approach to raising children. Raise both your sons and daughters as fully functional, well-rounded individuals; teach them all necessary life skills, be it cooking, doing the laundry, keeping the house clean or managing the household. Don't question a woman's ability to manage her home along with achieving professional success. Cheer equally for anyone doing well professionally in your family, be it your son, your daughter or your daughter-in-law. Only when we sow the seed of equality today will we reap the fruit of balanced lives in the future.

Instil in your children a sense of happiness for their being. Don't define their potential by their gender, end the passive messaging that a girl is inferior to a boy and that a girl needs to prove her worth time and again. Next time you hear the comment, 'What if she's a daughter, she's no less than a son', please stand up and correct the messaging. A woman is complete on her own. A high-achieving woman need not be compared to a man. It is important that we change this mindset. Let us not have our daughters grow up with the notion that every time they achieve something, they have finally matched up to being a son! Let them feel proud of who they are.

Bollywood actress Taapsee Pannu made a befitting comment that resonates with the spirit I'm trying to convey to my broader audience. On being called Bollywood's 'female Ayushmann Khurrana' by a producer, Taapsee beautifully retorted that she is, in fact, Bollywood's 'first Taapsee Pannu'.

#RainmakerSpeak

Raspreet Sidhu, captain of the Indian women's national basketball team

Give our girls wings to fly. Let them dream and let them believe in themselves.

—Raspreet Sidhu

Raspreet and I went to the same school. At the time, we were just acquaintances, but even today I can clearly recall her love and dedication for basketball. Just before our morning assembly, I would always see her practising with the girls' team, and after school hours, she would be back in the court, this time practising with the boys' team. Such was her persistence to excel. Years later, it came as no surprise when I read that she had made it big in professional basketball and was playing for India. She is, in fact, the only woman basketball player to represent India in three Asian Games. Among other firsts to her credit, she is the youngest female to have played for India in all three formats of the game: under-18, under-21 and the senior women categories.

Raspreet took to basketball at a time when the sport itself was not very popular in India, and there were not many girls who were popular figures in sports in general. When I started writing the book, Raspreet's name automatically came to mind, and I reconnected with her to learn about her journey of becoming the captain of the Indian women's basketball team, and as of today, the senior-most playing member of the team, with 16 years of experience.

Raspreet, let's start your journey with your love for the sport and how you evolved as a professional over time.

My journey with sports began when I was 12 years old. I have always been an athletic kid, inspired by my father who was a sportsman and used to represent his college. My father would do two hours of physical workout daily and I used to accompany him. As a kid, I have taken part in many sports—badminton, football, running—but when I took up basketball, I could feel a pull towards the game. My coach back then, V.P. Narula sir, made me realise my passion for basketball. He too had been a professional basketball player, and I looked up to him. Within a year I developed a great commitment for the game. When Narula sir moved to Montfort School, I moved schools, too, to continue getting trained by him, despite the fact that it meant a longer travel time for me. From then on, my routine would see me at school at 5 AM for basketball training, followed by classes during the regular school time and then a second practice session until 7 PM. My hard work paid off when I was selected for the Delhi State Championship at a very early age, and eventually, I played for the country for the first time when I was just 15, in the 10th grade. That was my turning point and I set my eyes on the blue jersey. Once I played for my country, I knew that this was what I was meant to do. Thus, love for the sport of basketball converted into the passion of playing for the country. Today, it's been over 16 years that I have been playing for the country and I feel very proud of it.

At the time when you took to professional basketball, there were not many female role models in sports. How did you decide to play basketball and what kept the motivation going? Who was your role model?

My father and my coach have been my role models. I learnt hard work and dedication from both of them. They both walked the talk when it came to perseverance. My father's mantra drives me even today as I continue to hold it close to my heart. He used to tell me that one can't achieve anything without hard work, and your hard work will never go to waste if you put your heart and soul into it. It is this advice that has gotten me so far.

My coach, V.P. Narula sir, also inspired me not only towards getting better at the game, but to also be a good student academically. He would always say that if you're not a good student then you're not a good player.

He was a gold medallist in chemistry, so he expected a certain level of academic performance from his players too. It was this conditioning that led me to focus on my studies and basketball in parallel. After school, I joined St. Stephen's College and graduated with a gold medal in physical studies from the University of Delhi.

Professionally, I have always looked up to the Japanese basketball player Yuko Oga and American basketball player, LeBron James. I also draw inspiration from Roger Federer, given his calm stance in the most stressful situations. He is always very respectful of his game. I have never seen him lose his cool whether he wins or loses, and that is a great quality to learn from.

Across different stages of your life, did you face any challenges in pursuing your sports journey?

As a child, I did not face any challenges in pursuing sports, and the credit for this goes to my gender-neutral upbringing. My father, in fact, encouraged the athlete in me. For me, academics and basketball went hand in hand. Even though I started playing for the country at a young age, I didn't drift away from academics, and this really helped me in the long run. As a national level player, when time commitment to the sport becomes full-fledged, it is the nation's responsibility to take care of its players by offering them job opportunities in government roles, banks, PSUs, etc. Unlike cricket and football, not much support is provided to women basketball players on this front, and this was my biggest challenge. While other sports get opportunities in multiple government organisations like ONGC, national banks, etc., we only have the railways as a major employment support option for women basketball players, and I did not see myself as a fit there. So, the looming question for me was to understand how to continue to play for the country and be financially secure at the same time. Fortunately, given my decent academic record and passion for sports, I got an opportunity to be the head of sports at Shiv Nadar School, which enabled me to keep playing at the national level.

To have a career of more than five years in sports, for women in India, is very remarkable. As time passes, physical and societal demands increase, there is the pressure to get married and raise children, and many women end up dropping sports as a career. The solution here is to have supportive parents, in-laws and, most importantly, solid support from your partner. Unless your partner respects you for who you are and what you have achieved so far, he won't be able to support your onward journey. I have been lucky in that department. Since my husband, Brahmaditya Singh, also belongs to the field of sports, he understands the demand of the game and what it means to represent the country. He is someone who would want to see the best version of myself on the court. He is also my trainer and my biggest critic, so his contribution to better my game is immense. Most importantly, he motivates and inspires me. My husband is the strong male counterpart I needed, someone who isn't threatened by my achievements. Both he and my in-laws are such confident people that they always encourage me to live my dream. But it is not so for every female athlete in India. Many of them do not marry because of the lack of respect for their game and their achievements, as men often feel emasculated by women's achievements.

What role can sports play as a gender equaliser?

Sports play a huge role here. From my own experience, it gives you an identity very early on. For instance, everyone in school knew me, the other kids looked up to me; I forged my own identity, which often women lack in India. Sports also develop confidence. My self-assurance on the court was visible in my life off the court, and I had the stamina to face anything and everything. Sports make you feel empowered and you feel no different than a man. Remember, we women are no less than men. The women's basketball team in India has done better than the men's team, and I take great pride in it. This is an empowering thought.

What would your advice be to parents and young girls in encouraging them for taking up sports as a career?

I would urge parents to disregard gender while raising their children. Expose your children, especially the girls, to some co-curricular activity, be it sports, art, dance, debate, etc. She will learn and achieve a lot more in life. So, in all, support your children to take up more than just studies. Be a supportive parent and let them decide what they want to do. Don't force your dreams on them. Give our girls wings to fly and the strength to believe in themselves. I always tell young children to dream on and dream big, put in the right amount of hard work and dedication and see your dreams turn into reality.

3

A for Assertive

We were taught to be dependable, responsible, the top of our classes at school, the most organized and efficient babysitters in town, the very miniature models of our hardworking farmer/nurse mother, a pair of junior Swiss Army knives, born to multitask.

—Elizabeth Gilbert
Journalist and author

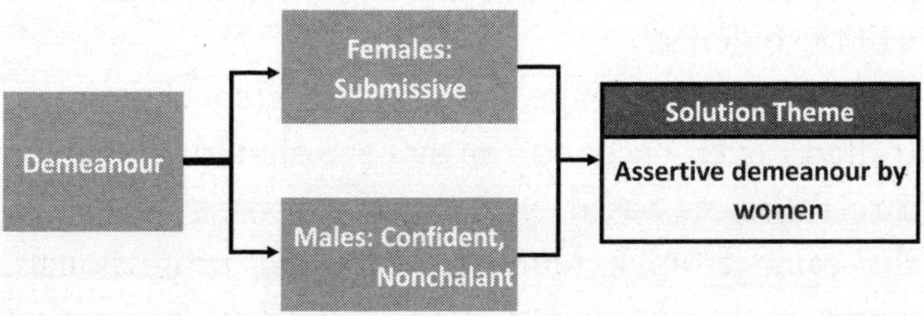

The demeanour and body language of women form another interesting aspect that shapes their career graph. Due to the deficiencies in upbringing, women tend to be more modest and self-effacing, and often ape the ways of the previous generation. Are we too scared to take a chance on our dreams and our ambitions? Probably so.

Let us understand this issue better by looking at a case study.

The Malhotras, a Delhi-based business family, have two sons—Aryan and Rohit. Both are the apple of their parents' eyes. Both sons are well-educated and smart, yet both chose very different life paths. While Aryan went to Bengaluru to pursue an MBA, Rohit decided to stay back and manage the family business. They got married a year apart.

Aryan married Anaya, his classmate from business school, a young and ambitious woman who started her career as a consultant in one of the big consulting think tanks. What attracted Aryan to Anaya was her zest for life and her confidence. They could have meaningful discussions, not just about personal matters, but also about their careers. Given that Anaya was much better at reading people and situations than him, Aryan would often ask her for advice on managing tricky work problems.

For Anaya, marriage was a happy personal moment. It didn't even occur to her that she should be making career choices based on her marital status—after all, she came from a family of working professionals, where both men and women boasted of decades of successful careers and family life. After marriage, Anaya and Aryan continued to stay in Bengaluru, and both managed their office work and home equally. Wherever they could rely on domestic help, they did so, and the other chores they did interchangeably as per each other's availability.

On the other hand, Rohit married Reema, his school-time sweetheart, who also happened to be the daughter of the Malhotras' close family friends. Reema's family was very different from Anaya's. In her family, only the men went out to work while the women solely took care of the household tasks.

Reema was academically strong and wanted to study economics abroad, but her parents made it clear that it was an implausible demand and that she should pursue another course closer home, one that was not as expensive. By their logic, at the end of the day, Reema would get married and manage her husband's home and for that, she didn't need expensive degrees. Reema, therefore, enrolled in a chartered accountancy programme. Having a sharp mind, she enjoyed the challenging course. She did really well and got a high all-India rank too.

Unlike Anaya's family, where her admission to an MBA was celebrated with much fanfare, Reema's rank did not impress her parents as much. Reema was instead appreciated when she cooked a perfect meal or when she made impeccable party arrangements for her mother. After completing her chartered accountancy degree, Reema was allowed to take up a job in her uncle's accounting firm. Despite being an all-India rank-holder, Reema did not apply to the big four audit firms, since she knew that she wouldn't be allowed by her parents to take up the opportunity. She was too scared to even try, justifying to herself that since she would be marrying Rohit soon, it would be a wasted effort.

As she began working at her uncle's accountancy firm, she realised how much she enjoyed her work. She was among the better performers at her workplace. As time flew by, her wedding came closer and her mother advised her to quit her job and focus on her upcoming life instead. She gave Reema her own example of how she wanted to be a designer and open her own boutique but decided otherwise after her marriage. Her mother expressed her concerns on how Reema wouldn't be able to stay happy while juggling too many things since after her marriage, all the household work would also be her responsibility. Rohit and his family's well-being would all lie on her shoulders. Reema was disappointed, but she took her mother's advice and quit her job.

The wedding was celebrated with gusto, and everybody got back to their usual routine once it was done. Anaya, Aryan and Rohit continued with their jobs while Reema got busy with domestic life. After a few months, Reema started missing her old routine—getting ready every morning for work and going out into the world, putting her qualification to good use. She felt she was becoming dull by the day. She continued to shoulder all the responsibilities of the house, but deep within herself, she was dissatisfied and unhappy.

The above case study shows how the chink in upbringing, and the resultant change in demeanour, creates multiple Reemas in India. Knowingly or unknowingly, we prevent our girls from realising their potential due to their gender. We bring them up with much love, we give them quality education, but we take away from them the confidence and the freedom to choose their own path. By putting blinders on them, we think that we are ensuring their happiness and guiding them towards a conflict-free life. But instead, we are leading them into a life of unfulfilled dreams, where they keep wondering what they could have accomplished had they been given a chance. Reema could be a happy homemaker if the decision was her own choice, not if she was forced to do so by fear or chose it under pressure.

Our upbringing plays a big role in shaping our behaviour. In Anaya's case, growing up in a family of professionals, she imbibed confidence, assertiveness and a sense of self-worth. She knew she was a complete person on her own and didn't feel the need to compromise on her career to take care of her husband's needs. Marriage was a partnership of equals for her—she had married a fully grown man and they would work together like a team. Anaya didn't put unnecessary pressure on herself by assuming that her husband was like a child who had to be taken care of by her. Whereas, in Reema's case, she saw how her mother single-handedly looked after the house—cooking, cleaning, doing the laundry, managing the domestic help, etc. She saw how her father would always get the last word on any household decision and, more often than not, he would not even consult his wife. Her mother also never expressed any ambition of her own; she just quietly and dutifully trod the path her husband laid. Thus, Reema went on to emulate what she had observed of her mother and resigned herself to a life of domesticity despite having great potential and intellectual prowess. She could not even conceive of her true potential, let alone realise it. Reema assumed that whichever path others chose for her would be the best option to follow. Some of it was due to her upbringing and some of it was her own outlook.

The looming question remains, how do we get out of this rut? How do we bring about the necessary change in our attitudes and ensure that the next generation is more equal and has the correct approach to valuing themselves and realising their dreams? To get some insights, I spoke with Japleen Pasricha, founder-director of Feminism in India (FII), a digital intersectional feminist media organisation with a million-plus followers. She's also a TEDx speaker and a UN World Summit Young Innovator.

Girls start well in academics, but a lot of them choose domesticity or a less strenuous career path as they grow up. What is the main reason for this, according to you?
Girls are generally brought up with the idea that even if they don't work, it is ok. They have the option of their father, and later their husband, providing for them. And even if they take up jobs, it is generally more stereotypical careers. For instance, many of my cousins are teachers not by their choosing, but because people perceived it to be an easy career path and they were guided towards it by their parents. It is not as easy for them either. They end up working eight to ten hours just like in any other job, whilst managing housework round the clock. But, given they are home by the time the kids are back from school, it is seen as a suitable career for women. This is where upbringing plays a major role; it is important to let each girl choose her own career unrestricted by gender.

As a child/young adult, were you signalled towards showcasing stereotypical feminine traits, like being coy and soft-spoken, by parents, relatives or teachers?

My mother is convent-educated and, therefore, she was quite conservative about our mannerisms. I was never traditionally effeminate; I would sit in whichever way I liked and talked and laughed loudly while my mom would expect me to sit properly, talk and laugh softly. She would mention how such unladylike behaviour at her school would be reprimanded. But I was always headstrong and believed in my own ways.

What can parents and the larger community do to ensure a gender-neutral upbringing?

Parents have a certain societal template in mind with which they raise kids. To their credit, they try to be supportive on many occasions, but then there are times when they fall into the shackles of society and pass on the societal pressure to their children. We are two sisters and often my relatives would comment on how our family is incomplete because we do not have a brother. In this case, my parents were resolute and would reply saying that we didn't need a boy to complete our family, as we were enough for each other.

Now, this was quite progressive of them, but fast forward to today and they have very different expectations from me and my sister. For instance, I have been doing really well with my start-up and recently moved to a bigger office. Soon after congratulating me, my mother's only concern was when will I plan a baby. This obviously will not be the reaction for my husband; he doesn't face such pressure. Therefore, we are still a long way from achieving gender neutrality. I guess it's now up to us to show gender equality to the children we raise, through our actions. Let us not have different standards for girls and boys and focus on giving them an equal education, independence and support so that they can pursue their calling.

Many women feel guilty when they pursue a career as they have to make sacrifices on the personal front. Have you observed the same? What would be your advice to them?

In the Indian scheme of things, husbands and the in-laws remain major stakeholders in the lives of married women. I would first advise the husband and the in-laws to support women in their professional pursuits because most women will not defy them. Also, parents need to support their daughters and instil in them the confidence that they can look up to them for support whenever needed (even after marriage). One important piece of advice to women—have a conversation about your professional ambitions with your partner and in-laws to get clarity before marriage. To me, financial independence for women is very important, irrespective of how rich your husband and your parents are. Love does not equal financial dependence.

My interaction with Japleen made one thing clear—we need to learn to be in the driver's seat in our own lives. Most women, knowingly or inadvertently, hand over the steering wheel of their lives to their parents first and their spouses and children later. In life, the majority of women are not driven by their passions and their capabilities, but by the baggage of responsibilities they carry towards their home and its members. Unless women question the status quo, they won't be able to bring about a change, and we need more and more women coming forth for equality to be achieved in the real sense. When there are relatable role models, successful, confident, high-achieving women to look up to, there will be an automatic change in the behaviour of the younger generation, who will turn out to be more assertive and confident. Look at Japleen. Despite her mother's concerns regarding her motherhood, she remains committed to her career. She chooses not to carry the extra pressure put on her because of her gender. Japleen, with her assertive demeanour and a go-getter attitude, is a role model to her team at the FII. Not only this, but she also mentors young women by offering voluntary mentoring services to fellows in various fellowship programmes. While these fellows have the domain knowledge, Japleen provides them with guidance and coaching so they can continue to chase their dreams.

For women, the road to professional success becomes progressively tough as the demands increase, both on the personal and the professional front, and this is where mentors and role models can play a very important role. This is something that I also relate to very closely. A lot of my academic and professional success is driven by strong women around me, especially my mother. Growing up, I could see my mother managing her family and her job beautifully, and that gave me the confidence that I too could find that balance in my life. My mom is a finance wizard; she's a Shri Ram College of Commerce alumna, a top-ranking college in India. She has made her career in the field of finance, a male-dominated domain, but she has successfully climbed the corporate ladder and has done well for herself. This laid a foundation for me to believe in myself and project a confident attitude. Thus, the right influences and encouragement in our childhood and the resultant confidence go a long way in enabling one to be the boss of their own life.

#RainmakerSpeak

Dr Rohini Godbole (Padma Shri, 2019), Indian physicist

'[Women] form almost 40% of the undergraduates in science … among the Ph.D.'s in science, about 25–30% are women … the proportion in faculty is around 15 and 20%, and at higher levels the number further drops.… Women heads of laboratories, science departments of the government, or as members of governing or advisory bodies are rare.'[1]

These numbers show that the leaky pipeline of women talent is not just limited to corporate India but is also visible in the field of STEM, research and academia.

> *…research is a highly creative and individualistic activity and each person makes his/her unique contribution. The process of scientific development, innovation and discovery can only benefit from diversity … given the fact that women are 50% of humanity, their intellectual potential is something that we can ill afford to ignore.*[2]
>
> —Rohini Godbole and Ramakrishna Ramaswamy

[1] https://www.ias.ac.in/public/Resources/Initiatives/Women_in_Science/AASSA_India.pdf

[2] https://www.ias.ac.in/public/Resources/Initiatives/Women_in_Science/AASSA_India.pdf

Dr Rohini Godbole is a trailblazer in the field of physics. She is a high-achieving particle physicist, best known for her theoretical work about explorations of physics of the elementary particles at particle colliders, such as the Large Hadron Collider (LHC) at CERN, European Organisation for Nuclear Research. She has been decorated with numerous awards and is the first woman physicist to be honoured with a Padma award (Padma Shri in 2019). In 2021, she has been awarded the Ordre national du Mérite, or the National Order of Merit, considered among the highest distinctions bestowed by France. She has authored more than 250 research papers and several graduate-level textbooks, and has mentored many students.

She is a true proponent of gender equality in the field of STEM and has worked relentlessly for over two decades to increase women's participation in science. She has initiated and co-edited books, such as *Lilavati's Daughters: Women Scientists of India* and *A Girls' Guide to a Life in Science*, which encourage young girls to pursue a career in science. She is one of the key persons who initiated the Gender in Physics Working Group (GIPWG) of the Indian Physics Association[3] and was the chair of the panel for Women in Science Initiative of the Indian Academy of Sciences.

[3] https://www.tifr.res.in/~ipa1970/news/godbolePadmashree.pdf

Family was and still is an important influencer

...it is not enough to talk to interested young girls; it is also important that they bring this problem to the attention of their fathers and the young men who may someday be their spouses. With their understanding and cooperation, [it all becomes so much easier].[4]

—Dr Rohini Godbole

At the start of my conversation with Dr Rohini, she reflected on her journey to becoming who she is today. She stressed how important it is to have a supportive family, especially for women, to be able to pursue a career.

'I come from a household where intellectual pursuits have always been encouraged. My mother was a teacher herself and I, along with my three sisters, had good family support for our education.

'While the family had a few doctors and engineers, there had been no scientists. But the support of my parents and family helped me explore things till I found out what I wanted. I did not know much about science and research in my initial journey, but my curiosity to learn new things, good friends I made and the supportive environment at home enabled the decisions with ease.

'I was not introduced to science till the seventh standard. It was only when I wanted to appear for the State Merit Scholarship that I started studying science. As I became one of the first students to win this scholarship from my school in many years, there was

[4] https://shethoughtit.ilcml.com/biography/rohini-godbole/

no looking back. I went on to do a BSc in physics from Pune and an MSc from IIT Mumbai. It was a coincidence that after completing my master's, I went to the US to finish my PhD. Post my PhD, I chose to come back to India. As I continued my journey as a scientist, I worked all over the world—labs in Germany, the US, Japan, etc., collaborating with scientists globally.

'My parents were supportive of all my choices despite some relatives and acquaintances warning my parents of the problems these could create for my marriage chances!'

Unconscious bias is like jealousy. Nobody likes to admit it and often we are unaware of it

'Biases creep in from a very early stage of your career—even from people who do not mean to undermine your capabilities. It reflects the biases we have about what a girl or a woman can or should do… the goals that she can or should set for herself? Let me give you some examples.

'My favourite teacher told me: "Why do you want to go abroad? We can find you a good place to do a PhD in India."

'One mentoring advice given to me: "Your best bet is to find a job in a women's college in a mofussil area."

'When I was a young researcher, I was told: "I never thought you were so serious about research!"

'I am not criticising the people who said these things, as they were all said in good faith. These could have been a reflection of their opinion about my academic abilities, but I do believe that my gender had some effect as well. To be honest, it is possible that any of these statements (had I taken them to my heart) could have stalled my career.

'Then there are some obvious biases at the workplace. Women scientists face several issues that stem from innate prejudice and bias, as well as patriarchal attitudes in the workplace. I have observed people saying things ranging from "Women lack mathematical and analytical capabilities" to "Women are a distraction in labs". Instances of such biases have reduced over time given the focus on gender sensitivity and more women working alongside their male counterparts, but there is still some way to go.'

A woman's life brings some really tough choices—age could be a bar

'As the years passed, my parents got increasingly worried about my marriage. But I was more focused on contributing to the field of science. Even today, most early-career grants/positions require candidates to be below 35/40 years of age. This limitation especially affects women as their biological clock and their career clock ticks simultaneously. Women need to make tough choices at this age, and many bright scientists drop off from their career path.

'I eventually did get married to a German colleague. But I postponed having children till the time that we both were in the same country or could find jobs that would have supported us in raising a family, but it never happened for us. Till today, I regret not having kids. However, I would be remiss if I don't mention the love and affection I get from my nephews and nieces which reduces this regret. Again (extended) family support helps!'

Being the change you want to see

'Please note that the aim is not necessarily to have an exact 50:50 representation across the branches. But one wants to create an atmosphere where merit rules and personal biases do not affect the choice of the person choosing and the advice that the mentors give.

'Reflecting back, I feel that if the institutions had more support measures, then women like me would not have to choose between having a family and pursuing a career. And to make it better for women now, we have included some recommendations in the Equity and Inclusion (E&I) charter that has been included in the draft of India's new Science, Technology, and Innovation Policy (STIP 2020), such as:

- Tenure clock extension policies for women who need it due to childbirth—this would ensure a level playing field for promotions.
- Having at least 30 per cent women scientists on all panels such as recruitment drives, budget allocation, and promotion and tenure committees. The active presence of women on such panels will lead to more inclusive decision-making.
- Compulsory training and workshops at regular intervals for all staff and faculty members to address

any conscious or unconscious biases and make the workplace a gender-inclusive place.

- Instituting mentorship programmes and support networks for women in STEM in all organisations. This guidance and support are especially needed in the early career of a woman.

'The list is not exhaustive, but the idea is to create a level playing field by ensuring the biological differences between the two genders are respected and inclusion focus is shared across all relevant stakeholders. Through all these efforts, I want to leave a better world for women to pursue their passions. This not only benefits women but it also benefits that particular field of study/ profession. I say this many times—if we lose a woman scientist in the middle of her career, it's a huge loss for science too! Imagine the progress she could have made if she had been given the right support.'

To sum up, as Dr Rohini Godbole and Dr Ramakrishna Ramaswamy write in their report, 'Women Scientists in India', for the Association of Academies and Societies of Sciences in Asia (AASSA), India, 'The importance of mainstreaming gender in all walks of life cannot be over-emphasized. This is not just to make sure that women get a chance to give expression to their creativity and abilities but also because it is essential for the balanced development of any society.'[5]

[5] https://www.ias.ac.in/public/Resources/Initiatives/Women_in_Science/AASSA_India.pdf

4

Shaping Up with Role Models

Define success on your own terms, achieve it by your own rules, and build a life you're proud to live.
—Anne Sweeney
Former co-chair, Disney Media Networks

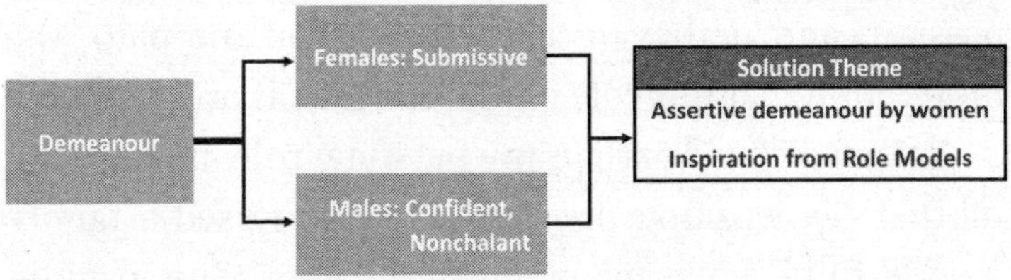

Beyond an ideal upbringing, introspecting on what is important and having an assertive behaviour are necessary to achieve the freedom to make personal life choices. The way one projects an assertive attitude depends on the life stage one is at. For instance, a child's behaviour is greatly influenced by their parents. But they can also be influenced to a great extent by the right role model, someone they can look up to, learn from and emulate in life. On the other hand, young adults who have passed this stage need to define their own rules on how they conduct themselves in society, and while they do this, a role model can motivate them to pursue their ambition and give them the strength to face challenging situations. When we see people we admire achieve heights of success, it gives us the courage and hope to pursue our dreams.

Role models are to children what targets are for a sale team: Motivation to do more

From a young age, parents should actively guide their children towards looking up to and emulating a role model. Of course, this role model can change with time, as the child grows up. But having an idol can go a long way in helping children work relentlessly towards their passion, and if they face challenges on the path, the motivation that this role model can give is unparalleled.

As I mentioned earlier, my personal role model is my mother—a working professional who raised a family wonderfully while managing her career. She inspired me to be an ambitious woman myself. From her, I learned to pursue my passion in parallel with having a family. She always planned her days meticulously, leveraging help from my grandparents, father, domestic help and crèche facilities. In later years, when my sister and I were in our teens, she trusted us to be competent enough to take care of ourselves. She always knew how to manage every aspect of her life; she was the Wonder Woman I had around me at every phase of my life. Following her path, I too entered the world of finance. Her success inspired me and pushed me to give my best academically.

It is refreshing to see that now women have several female role models in various fields—academics, sports and business—of which there was a dearth earlier. For instance, I have noticed in recent years that cricket in India is gaining traction among young girls, with the successive exemplary performances of our women's team. This has led to many girls looking up to Mithali Raj (captain of the Indian women's national cricket team) as their role model and in pursuing professional cricket. Such idols are not just limited to cricket. Badminton has P.V. Sindhu and Saina Nehwal, tennis has Sania Mirza, athletics has Dutee Chand and Hima Das and boxing has Mary Kom, among other shining examples. We are now seeing more girls taking up sports professionally and harbouring ambitions of representing India internationally one day.

To see an admirable and relatable role model shattering the glass ceiling and creating records gives many others the firepower and motivation to attempt it too. Typically, people get inspired to do something when they see others do it. When women see other women in successful roles, they find it easier to aspire to the same heights. Seeing more women in leadership positions will not only encourage others, but also make their parents, their peers and the larger community aware of the immense possibilities open to young girls. But it is not just female idols who can inspire women—men can be role models too! A role model should not be picked on the basis of their gender. Cricketer Shafali Verma became the youngest Indian to hit an international half-century at the age of 15. By hitting this 50, she broke the 30-year-old record of Sachin Tendulkar, who was 16 when he hit his first test half-century. Interestingly, Shafali's professional role model is Sachin Tendulkar.

Her personal inspiration and support has been her father, who wanted to become a cricketer himself but could not because of family pressures. Similarly, Sheryl Sandberg's professional role model is Mark Zuckerberg, just as Warren Buffett is the role model for several women who want to be amazing investors and great leaders.

Male leaders who understand the importance of workplace diversity and encourage it are also an inspiration, a positive reinforcement to give wings to ambitions.

You're young only once: Paint the vistas, take chances and be proud

As a young woman, make your choices freely. Pursue your dreams—you may want to get out in the world or you may be someone whose happiness lies in staying home. The key is to make your own choices, free of any guilt, and not to fall in the die-cast of society's expectations.

An advertisement campaign by Titan Raga demonstrates the same point beautifully. A confident woman struggles to make a choice between her career and the chance to have a family because the man she falls in love with feels emasculated by her success. He wants her to quit her job to move forward in their relationship. The woman proudly makes herself her priority and chooses her aspirations over marriage. The advert moves along to show the woman's peaceful and dignified manner over time, while the man is still stuck in his dogmatic ways.

Climb heights and inspire on

We have seen the importance role models have for the younger generation; they can motivate and give courage to millions to pursue their dreams. A role model can be an inspiration at any age, be it a teenager, a young mother or even someone in their golden years. Sania Mirza is not only an icon for young girls and aspiring tennis players, but also for married women and new mothers who get motivated by seeing her preparations for a comeback after motherhood. I am reminded of the instance where veteran journalist Rajdeep Sardesai, while interviewing Sania Mirza, asked her about her plans of settling down. Sania's response to this won many hearts and was widely lauded. She replied, 'You sound disappointed that I'm not choosing motherhood over being number one in the world at this point of time. But I'll answer your question anyway, that's the question I face all the time as a woman, that all women have to face—the first is marriage and then it's motherhood. Unfortunately, that's when we're settled, and no matter how many Wimbledons we win or number ones in the world we become, we don't become settled.' Rajdeep subsequently apologised to Sania and also admitted that he wouldn't have asked this question to a male athlete.

The show business is one that holds the imagination of most, especially the youth. We are a movie-obsessed country that holds its stars in complete awe and admiration. Young men and women emulate these actors and the characters they play. Therefore, it is an important medium to influence young minds. In this regard, a section of the Indian film fraternity deserves credit in trying to create female-centric content, even taking the storyline to the hinterlands. Beautiful stories of inspiring, high-achieving, valorous women have been told through recent movies. These stories would not have reached the masses had it not been for mainstream commercial cinema. Each of these films talks about the lives of iconic women, whether it is *Dangal*, telling the story of female wrestlers Geeta Phogat and Babita Phogat, *Saand Ki Aankh* inspired by Chandro Tomar and Prakashi Tomar, two of the oldest sharpshooter champions in the world, *Panga*, the story of a professional kabaddi player who makes a comeback after motherhood, or *Neerja*, the story of Neerja Bhanot, a flight attendant who died saving passengers from terrorists on a hijacked flight. These achievers are finally getting their due after the movies based on their stories reached the masses, motivating thousands of young girls and women to chase their dreams bravely outside of society's conventions.

It's never too late to pursue your passion

For the current generation of young women, I say that you must learn to be confident in your own life choices, to value yourself for the contribution you make by either staying at home or by stepping out. Be the change you want to see in the world.[1] You are the only person who can change your life. The change will come about slowly, one day at a time; don't lose hope. Eventually,

[1] Quote by Mahatma Gandhi.

you will learn to love yourself and to value your dreams. Just like you work relentlessly for your family, you have to find the motivation in yourself to work for your dreams. Make your own choices from a position of self-belief, not as a compromise or because somebody else made the choice for you. There's simply no age barrier to do this! You may be a young woman just starting out, in your 30s and 40s, married with young kids or even older, with years of wisdom behind you. Take that first step in the journey of valuing yourself and pursuing your passion.

As a dose of inspiration for all the ladies, let me cite the example of Sudha Murthy, wife of Narayan Murthy, the founder of the multibillion-dollar IT company Infosys. Sudha devoted some of her best years to her husband's dream and to raising her children. She did so despite her strong academic credentials and a thriving career at Telco (now Tata Motors), where she was the first woman engineer. Sudha gave it all up to move to Pune to support her husband in his journey of founding Infosys. It wouldn't have been a surprise if Sudha had gotten lost in her husband's accomplishments, but there was a spark in her as she made strides in carving out her own identity. Sudha took up teaching, and by the time she was 45 years of age, she was the head of department (HoD) of computer science at Bengaluru University. During this time, she also explored her love for writing and became a bestselling author. As a notable philanthropist and chairperson of Infosys Foundation, she has helped open 60,000 libraries, several new schools and over 16,000 washrooms in India. She is the recipient of the R.K. Narayan Award for Literature and the prestigious Padma Shri award from the Government of India. As a woman and as a mother, I draw great motivation from Sudha's life, her philosophies, her passion and the superb balancing act with which she runs her life. Today, she stands tall in stature not just as a devoted wife and mother, but also as a high-achieving, compassionate individual who is doing so much for the betterment of society.

Another phenomenal lady, whose story I would like to share here, is Katharine Graham (16 June 1917–17 July 2001), who was the US's first female Fortune 500 CEO, holding the position at *The Washington Post* for 18 years, from 1972 to 1991. Today she is remembered as one of the most influential women of her time, who led *The Washington Post* to formidable success. But her journey started very differently as she assumed the role of a homemaker right after her marriage to Phil Graham. While Phil focused on his career, Katharine took care of their children. It was only in 1963, after the death of her husband, that she took over as the president of the Washington Post Company. The transition was not easy; there were many people who exploited her gender-related self-doubt and tried to convince her to not take over the publication house. But drawing from her inner strength and instinct, she ignored the naysayers and took over at the helm of the company. She was around 46 years old then.

Such inspiring stories prove how strong and remarkable women are. We just need to channel our strength towards our passions as well. Maintaining a family and raising children is not an easy task, but if you have within yourself a desire to work or to pursue a career, then disregard age and stage of life as a barrier and remember the stories of these incredible women. They will light up that fire in your belly which will help you in carving your individual identity.

She remembered who she was and the game changed.
—Lalah Delia
Artist and writer

5

The Choice Pickle and Its Solution

Women are the largest untapped reservoir of talent in the world.
—Hillary Clinton
Lawyer and politician

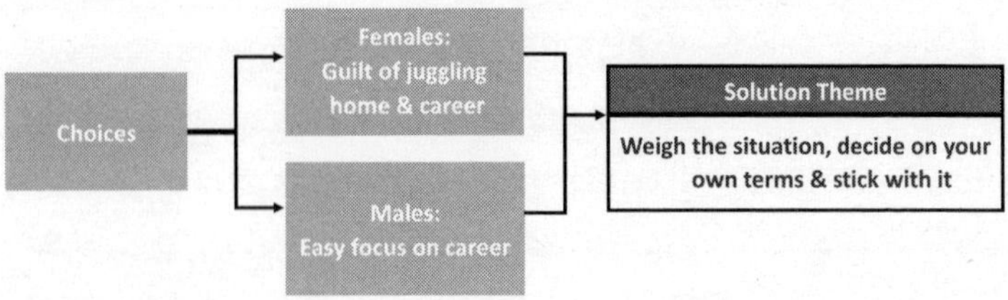

A woman's life is all about making choices, especially when you approach marriage and motherhood. You may be at any level of your career, but the pressure of choosing between your family and your work is one that will persist daily. An interview by Indra Nooyi highlights this very point. As the former CEO of one of the US's largest Fortune 500 beverage companies, PepsiCo, she too was not immune to the whirlwind of choices. Nooyi acknowledged that 'it's "rarely possible" to be the perfect mother, wife and worker at the same time. Understanding this conflict is the first step to finding solutions.... Important too, is understanding that each choice is its own sacrifice and that it will be impossible to "have it all".'[1]

As a woman, your life can look quite different based on the choices you make. There are three broad paths which we can choose from:

- A full-time homemaker
- A part-time professional
- A full-time professional

Hail the homemaker! Taking up the only 24x7 job in the world

It takes commitment, patience and humility to run the house and take care of its members selflessly. The amount of multitasking involved is truly unparalleled.

The job description of a homemaker demands a lot more than what is imaginable. It involves:

- Working 24 hours without any pay or leave
- Being an all-round supervisor: manage health and education, household operations (from food to cleaning), marketing and investor relations (everything from domestic help to socialising with friends and family) and household finances
- Working with limited recognition and appreciation

For full-time homemakers and mothers, managing a house and raising children—the future of the world—is

[1] https://www.cnbc.com/2018/10/03/indra-nooyi-shares-a-work-regret-on-her-last-day-as-pepsico-ceo.html

no mean feat. We see so many people crediting their success to their mothers and their wives, who function as the backbone of their children and husbands respectively. Without the devotion and self-sacrifice of these women, the world would have missed out on many successful and great achievers.

In an interview with the *New York Times,* investor and real estate mogul Barbara Corcoran explained how her mother, a homemaker who raised 10 children, was a role model for her. Barbara learnt multiple life lessons from her: to plan things well and be organised while multitasking, have positive energy and attitude to help you wade through any problem, to always be compassionate and focus on the bright side of situations and that sometimes tough love helps you learn more in life. Barbara says, 'I took to management like a duck to water. It was in my blood. Every single thing I've done is just a business version of what my mom did on the home front.'[2]

Closer home, P.V. Sindhu, the most prolific Indian badminton player today, dedicated the gold medal she won at the 2019 BWF World Championships to her mother, whose birthday was coincidentally on the same day. Sindhu's mother, Vijaya, who herself was a volleyball player representing the notable Railways team, chose to take voluntary retirement from her job in the Indian Railways to focus on her daughter's upbringing and career. Vijaya has been a pillar of strength for Sindhu at all times, ensuring a healthy environment for her to

[2] https://www.nytimes.com/2017/06/02/business/barbara-corcoran-shark-tank.html?src=me&_r=2

grow in, both physically and mentally. P.V. Sindhu acknowledges her mother's invaluable contributions in establishing her career: 'My mother's role cannot be quantified and measured. Simply put, if not for her, I couldn't have had this kind of a career.'[3]

These examples, and many other unknown stories, are a testimony to the important role of a homemaker. Without her support, the family will not be able to operate and perform to its full potential. Their contribution to society is beyond quantification for GDP contribution. And while we wait for society to put an economic value to homemakers, I would like to grab your attention to a remarkable point made by economist and Nobel Laureate Paul Krugman:

> I don't mean to imply that there's something wrong with more women working, but gain in family income that occurs because a spouse goes to work isn't the same thing as a wage increase. In particular, it may carry hidden costs that offset some of the gains in money income, such as reduced time to spend on housework, greater dependence on prepared food, day-care expenses, and so on.[4]

Aligned with the point presented by Paul Krugman, a 2004 study in the *American Economic Review* found that the motivation and support a wife provides to her husband increases his commitment to the job and

[3] https://www.olympicchannel.com/en/stories/features/detail/pv-sindhu-parents-pv-ramana-vijaya-indian-badminton-player-volleyball/

[4] https://lifebeyondnumbers.com/housewife-time-to-change-the-outlook-of-this-underrated-and-thankless-job/

boosts his income by about 27 per cent. This amounts to about US$1 trillion of combined salaries, which can be attributed entirely to the support husbands receive from their wives. Additionally, the benefits of a stay-at-home mother become all the more evident when one factors in the positive effects it has on children.[5]

Therefore, if one chooses to be a homemaker, it should be remembered that they are making an immense contribution to the present and the future of the country. The important thing to bear in mind is that this choice should be made by women on their own terms and not by coercion or societal pressures.

They can, because they think they can!

The next category of women comprises those who have family commitments but want to do something in addition to their household work. Let's look at a case study to understand women who strive to find a balance between working part-time and managing their household responsibilities with equal respect.

Natasha was born in a traditional Delhi family. Though her parents educated both their son and daughter equally, Natasha did not have the freedom to pursue a career. In her early 20s, she was married off to the only son of a well-to-do business family. All that was expected of her was to take care of the three family members (her mother-in-law, father-in-law and

[5] https://www.thetrumpet.com/16255-how-homemakers-help-the-economy

husband), look pretty, attend extended family parties and functions and, in time, become a mother. Natasha knew all this before getting married and she happily chose this life for herself.

But after a few months of being married, once the honeymoon phase was over, she realised that she found it tough to sit idle at home the whole day. Living in an affluent family, with only a few adult members to look after and enough domestic help, her days were quite empty. Natasha felt that her life was in a rut.

This was when she decided to remedy the situation, but she knew the constraints she was working with. She was determined to find a solution and give meaning to her life while operating within the limitations she had. Natasha was aware that she wouldn't be able to do a regular job; going to the office daily was not an option for her. She also knew that she had to devote the required hours to household chores—cooking three meals a day, overseeing the house help in all the daily tasks and also regularly attending family parties, of which there were far too many, given the large size of her extended family. Thus, she carefully defined her operating field and started looking for solutions that would be right for her.

She also discussed the matter with her husband, who was quite supportive. He especially praised Natasha's efforts to look for a solution within the circumstances. One night, while Natasha and her husband were having a discussion, he had an epiphany! He got up excitedly and asked Natasha if she wanted to try her hand at stock trading. Her husband, who worked at an accounting firm, was himself an avid stock investor.

Natasha had never traded in stocks before, but her husband was more than happy to guide her. He helped her start by providing a reading list for basic stock trading books. He also got her on a few mailing lists for research reports that he regularly read to make his trading calls.

Natasha was quite enthused and woke up with excitement the next morning. She completed her morning chores and started reading the material provided by her husband quite voraciously. She also started watching business news channels for the entire duration of the trading hours, from 9:30 AM to 3:30 PM. In between her readings and watching the news, she would step out of her room to finish her household tasks.

In the evening, when her husband came home, he could see the sparkle in Natasha's eyes. She gleefully told him all that she had read during the day. Natasha continued with this routine for three months. She read everything she could lay her hands on. She now knew that she agreed with trading based on the fundamental analysis method versus the technical analysis one. Warren Buffett's style of value investing made an impression on her in a big way.

As her husband saw the consistency with which Natasha showed interest in stock trading, he went ahead and opened a demat account for her. Natasha was always a smart one when it came to money. In less than six months after starting with stock trading, Natasha had built an impressive portfolio.

What does Natasha's story tell us?

She was a bored housewife who could have spent her whole life complaining about the circumstances she once happily chose for herself. But instead of falling into a rut, Natasha decided to look at the situation constructively and found the most practical and balanced way out for herself.

In life, we often need to find solutions for our problems within the circumstances we are dealt with. Lamenting your situation and making comparisons with others who may have, for instance, more liberal in-laws or supportive partners is not productive. We each have it within ourselves to find a purpose in our lives that brings us fulfilment. Like Natasha, you too can work around your own situation and find that balance you seek. It does require some peaceful deliberation and consistency of action, but it is ultimately obtainable.

There are many more inspiring stories of women similar to Natasha's. With ready access to the digital world, you can get trained in most disciplines from the comfort of your home. Whether your interest lies in beauty and cosmetics, cooking and baking, teaching, writing or any other vocation, go ahead and learn to utilise the power of social media platforms to market your products. There are many women-led SMEs (small and medium-sized enterprises) that have emerged under similar circumstances. Today, there are several Natashas who are bloggers, social media influencers, online teachers and entrepreneurs, among others.

#RainmakerSpeak

Chhavi Mittal, actor, YouTuber, influencer, co-founder of Shitty Ideas Trending (SIT), founder of *Being Woman with Chhavi*

To get insights into the opportunity that the digital world offers women and how its evolution has worked for women both as service providers and as consumers, I leapt at the opportunity of talking to Chhavi Mittal, a much-loved actor, YouTuber, influencer and content creator. Chhavi, along with her husband Mohit Hussein, has co-founded SIT, a digital production company, which has been recognised as one of the top content creators of India and has over seven million followers across platforms. She is also the founder of *Being Woman with Chhavi*, a YouTube channel where she shares content and advice on pregnancy, parenting, fitness and healthcare. Today, Chhavi reaches millions of people and has strung a great balance between her personal and professional lives. Here are the excerpts of our interaction.

Motivation to move to digital

'The motivation was definitely starting a family. I realised that television required both Mohit and I to work 12 to 13 hours a day plus travel time. This meant that we wouldn't have any time to spend with the child. For us, starting a family was not just about having a child but to build a life with the child. As parents, it is our responsibility to do justice to the life we bring into this world and that (to us) meant spending quality time with the child. We felt being with our child would enable better mental and emotional growth. This guided us towards the digital world. But the journey was gradual.

'When I had my first child, my daughter Areeza, we were still figuring things out. It was always an either/or working situation for Mohit and me since one of us had to be with the baby. And in the first two years, it was broadly me being at home since I was a first-time mother and was very protective of her. Then, gradually I started stepping out and Mohit had to be at home to be with her. This is when we realised that we wanted a better system that gives both of us the flexibility of being with our kids, and that is when the idea of going digital and starting our own platform with SIT came to us. Honestly, it was the best way forward, it gave us the freedom to plan our time and attend to both personal and professional commitments in parallel.'

A changed world for women

'Women are definitely a large part of the digital world today. The numbers may be below the global average, but we are seeing good traction now. There are many women coming on social media as influencers, some are selling consumer products and many are content creators. Today, there are many women as part of the audience. For instance, SIT, which has gender-neutral content, has 65–70 per cent women as followers. I take great comfort in this fact that the content I am creating is reaching more women. It is truly the need of the hour to have more women on social media to share their points of view and to consume more content. When your consumer base evolves, the content evolves too—it is all about who you are catering to with your content. More women as consumers means more gender-sensitive content. This has led to many women exploring digital platforms as a career path.'

Talking about women as consumers of digital media, she said, 'Online content answering doubts of women on a plethora of matters like conceiving, pregnancy, parenting, career guidance, health issues, etc., has proved to be really helpful. The generation before ours did not have the luxury to share their doubts and have them answered without the fear of judgment. Online content has helped a great deal in the education of women in a way. I focus on making a community where everyone's opinions are respectfully heard and there is a healthy discussion on matters rather than one person commanding other women on what is right and what is wrong. Imagine the strength of such a community which is rooted in mutual respect and freedom of opinion.'

Advice for women who want to pursue digital as a career path

'It is a great career path if you are passionate about it. Focus is important as that determines your approach. It depends on how you want to use a digital platform—do you want to be a content creator or do you want to sell consumer products (like cosmetics, accessories, customised gifts and bakery, etc.). I see a lot of women becoming entrepreneurs through social media. Many women-led businesses have flourished by just being an Instagram page. The growth potential is amazing!

'As you pursue your digital journey, define some key performance indicators (KPIs) for yourself—clear objective benchmarks help. For example, if you are a content creator, then your focus should be on numbers—number of subscribers, number of followers, number of likes and comments. But if you are selling products, then focus on sales and not just on the number of followers or subscribers. You need to focus on the end result you want.'

Gender-agnostic nature of social media

As my discussion with Chhavi moved ahead, I noted how the corporate world had men outnumbering women across levels and I wanted to get her views on the kind of paradigm social media had evolved into. This is what she had to say, 'Thankfully on social media, I have seen that as long as what you are doing is appealing to your audience, you are in a good place. It does not really matter whether, as a content provider, you are a man or a woman. You have to focus on who your target audience is. For instance, if you are creating gender-centric content or age-centric content (say for teenagers), what is relevant is the appeal to that target audience; gender will not create an impediment. Also, social media has definitely given a voice to everybody. A lot of women who find it difficult to voice their opinions in day-to-day life find it easier to get an outlet on social media, and this helps them channelise their own energy. Social media is also a place where people forget easily, they move on to the next thing. So, even if you commit a mistake, a second chance comes much faster than in real life, hence you can experiment more.'

Moving ahead

'As I made the switch from television to digital and eventually expanded the scope of my work from SIT to further include *Being Woman* in the scheme of my work, I am quite pleased with the choices I have made. I took my time to decide the way ahead for me, had a supporting partner in my husband along the way and took the leap. By doing so, I also feel good about the fact that my husband and I are setting up a good example for our children—Areeza and Arham. Both my daughter and my son know that they are equals, with gender being an irrelevant metric in determining what they want to do in life. Through my conduct, I especially want my daughter to know that it is completely fine to recalibrate the direction of one's life as per the need of the time. We don't have to be stuck in any societal template.'

After talking to Chhavi, I could further reaffirm one thing—whether you choose to be a full-time homemaker, an all-out career woman or a part-time worker, be happy with your choice and stop second-guessing your decisions. Doing so will go a long way in closing the gap between a man's and a woman's life graph.

#RainmakerSpeak

Reeba Chacko, partner (head corporate), Cyril Amarchand Mangaldas

I am assertive when a situation demands but I choose my battles. If along the way, I have to make any tough decisions, I make them on my own terms.
—Reeba Chacko

One of the key questions most women face is a potential career break at the advent of motherhood. To answer this, let me draw upon the conversation I had with Reeba Chacko, a renowned corporate lawyer who is a partner and head of corporate practice at Cyril Amarchand Mangaldas (CAM). Reeba has extensive experience of over 20 years with private equity clients globally. She has numerous awards and industry recognition to her credit.

I asked Reeba about her journey and how she made her choices.

'I had my child when I was in my late 20s. I decided to take a year off from work then, a longer-than-usual maternity break, and rejoined work post the year break. I also decided to take another year off when I decided to pursue higher studies, again a personal choice that I felt I wanted to explore at that stage in my life. I returned to my firm after both my breaks, but I never burdened myself with the thought that because of the break, I would fall behind my peers in my career. And I did not in the long term. I owned my decision and never doubted it.

I was happy because I had made this choice on my own terms.

'As a professional and as a mother, I make daily choices. For instance, I have always stayed close to my office. To stay in the heart of Bengaluru in the initial years of my career was an expensive proposition, but I took that call so I could manage work and my child more easily. Around the time of my son's exams, I would say no to opportunities that would deprive my young son of my presence like those involving foreign travel. Even today, if my grown son needs me, I choose to be with him at the cost of an opportunity… some mothers like me, whether right or wrong, would say there are times in a child's life when they need a mother more than anyone else. At these times, I make a choice to be with him and in doing so, if I have to let go of opportunities at work, then I do it without fretting or fighting for alternatives or flexibilities. And these situations differ at different stages of one's life. And may be different from person to person.

'Looking back, all my choices have served me well. I have made many choices, including for the sole reason that I am a woman, but I have been, and I still am, happy to make them. I have not felt that I have had to make compromises that I have not been happy about. I found my peace, happiness and success (in my own eyes at least) despite the choices or compromises.

'So, this is my advice to all the ladies, unhesitatingly make your choices at every turn in your life. The road ahead will get easier with time and experience, and it will all be worth it. There's no point in revisiting or regretting your choices or compromises, as long as you make them on your terms. Let go a little sometimes. Everything is about finding a balance. Be assertive while choosing what suits you best. With no fear of going wrong. And then you mostly get it right.'

To sum up my conversation with Reeba on this aspect, two words stand out: refreshing and practical. One particular thought that resonates so well with mine and is true for everybody irrespective of their gender is this—choose your battles. Biases are a part of human nature, and while there is an effort being made to make people aware of their biases, there is a limited point in being burdened by them. Thus, don't give in to the pressure of being judged for your choices. How Reeba approached her break or how she makes her choices in everyday work seems perfect—she doesn't overthink and she certainly doesn't feel victimised by biology. I can relate to this personally too. When I decided to leave my day job to focus on my pregnancy and pursue my passion for writing on gender inclusion, I didn't overthink what my peers or seniors may say. I knew in my heart what I wanted to do and I went for it.

Life is a matter of choices, and every choice you make makes you.

—John C. Maxwell

American author, speaker and pastor

6

Approaching the Corporate World

Alone we can do so little; together, we can do so much.
—Helen Keller
Author and political activist

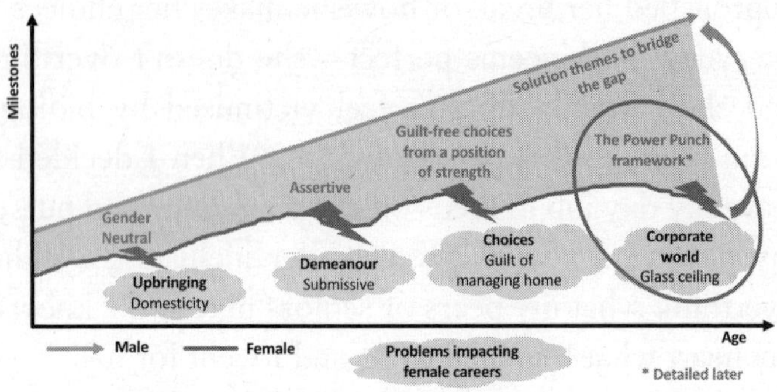

Let's talk about professional women, the ones who have decided that their career goals are above and beyond any household responsibility. With a lot of commitment, they have overcome mental, emotional and societal barriers to become financially and socially independent. However, is life all rosy for them? Not quite.

For most women who are focused on their career, marriage does not hinder their professional growth, but motherhood brings with it different problems. A guilt spiral sets in. We will get to the part of companies handling maternity breaks later in the book, but first, let's focus on the psyche and the behaviour of the woman herself.

Becoming a mother is a beautiful moment, an indescribable feeling. However, for many professional women, the pressures after becoming a mother become tough to handle. She gets torn between being with her child and doing her job. Her choices include:

- Becoming a stay-at-home mother
- Taking a career break of a few years
- Joining back work on finishing her maternity leave

Although it is two people who have a baby together, the burden of parenthood and the associated guilt with going back to work lie mostly with the woman. Before making life-changing decisions, women must learn to tackle their guilt and let go a little. Since a husband and wife both become parents together, it would then make sense to share the responsibilities that come with the baby. Uneven distribution of household work is an important underlying issue that needs to be addressed. Simply getting women back to offices doesn't win the equality crusade if they lack the support from their partners, parents and in-laws in creating a remarkable career. Equal participation is needed from all members of the family to share the load and run the house seamlessly so that the upbringing of the next generation is not compromised. Life is easier when we have the support of our loved ones. We are able to become the best version of ourselves with help from them. Most women with supportive families continue with their careers with greater ease.

The most important enabler for women is a support system on which they can rely guilt-free. Your partner, parents-in-law, parents and you need to work as a team, dividing responsibilities and taking full accountability for fulfilling these responsibilities. This team needs to support and nurture one another and step into each other's shoes in tricky or demanding situations. If you don't take this approach, you will end up harming yourself, both professionally and personally. It will become difficult for you to give 100 per cent at the workplace, which in turn will make you increasingly dissatisfied. At a personal level, you may end up trying to overcompensate at home by doing it all on your own. Therefore, before deciding on anything, first be at peace in your heart and set your dream team in place for the little one.

If you choose to be a stay-at-home mom, then take pride in it. You may take some time in adjusting to your new routine, but if you've made this choice on your own, unrestricted by the burden of your family, then you will be happy.

If you plan to take a career break of a few years, then accept the fact that once you decide to join back, you may have to start at the same level that you left at. But don't be disheartened; just do your best and be assertive. You will get back on track sooner than you expect. During the career break, keep yourself updated with the developments in your field of work; continue to upskill yourself by pursuing relevant courses. If your timetable permits, you can even take on consulting assignments that may come your way.

For those who plan on joining work immediately after their maternity leave, don't feel guilty for choosing to step out. Believe in your choice and your preparation. As a mother, you have given your best and arranged for a great caregiving team to look after the baby, be it the father, the grandparents, a nanny or a childcare centre. Always remember, a happy woman makes a better mother, and when your children grow up, you will be a role model for them.

Once this shift in the mindset of women happens and the smooth functioning of the family is accomplished, resolving biases in the corporate world will become easier.

Women need to accept the fact that motherhood will bring with it a lot of changes. But this doesn't mean you put too much pressure on yourself to keep circumstances around you unaffected. Some things you can plan for, and some others you will figure out as you move ahead in life. The little human in your life will require attention, and that will mean extra personal work and some time off from your professional work. There will be a lot of naysayers who may raise doubts, but don't let that define your course of action. Don't let others dictate what you should or should not be doing. Make your own support system; discover what works and what doesn't work for you, by yourself.

Give yourself some time to get used to the new realities of your life, and in the process, get all the help you deserve, not just from your family but from your organisation too. Accept the fact that you do have the added responsibility of a child, but this doesn't mean that you hold off your professional life. Don't try to do it all alone because you won't be able to do justice to any of it and will tire in an attempt to juggle everything. That is when the guilt spiral sets in—when you try to overcompensate at home and become disoriented at work.

The solution to this problem is twofold.

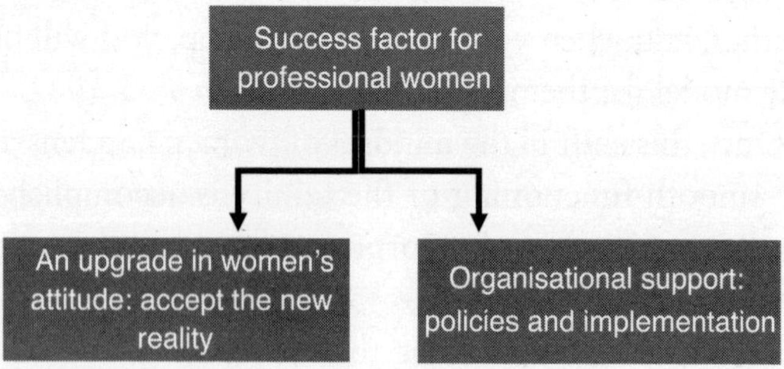

The numerous discussions I have had with new mothers have made it evident that, to begin with, women need to change their own mindset and attitude. Accepting your new reality and seeking help from your family and organisation to cope best with your change in circumstances are the way forward. Don't give in to pressure, voice your concerns freely and make your own choices. To highlight the issue better, let me present accounts of two women I spoke with.

My friend Samara works as an HR manager at an IT firm in Bengaluru. Her family and in-laws live in Surat, a thriving town in Gujarat. Samara put off having a child till she was 32 years old, focusing instead on reaching a certain level in her career. When she got pregnant, she was certain that she would want to continue with her job. At the same time, she was aware that she would need help from her family, and since they were in a different city, some pre-planning was needed. Her mother-in-law was quite accommodative and came to Bengaluru for Samara's delivery and spent the first two months there with her grandchild. While Samara was on maternity leave, she travelled to Surat so the baby could spend time with the extended family. Five months flew by quickly and the day to rejoin the office drew closer.

When Samara shared her decision to go back to work, her close relatives were not very kind to her. Very quickly she was labelled a heartless mother, more focused on making money than being devoted to her child. Though she was hurt, Samara was clear in her mind and had already planned for the imminent change. She knew that her organisation had a day-care facility within the office premises where she planned on keeping her daughter. Samara could easily check on her as many times as she wanted to, and she could also breastfeed her during the day. There would be many other children of her daughter's age at the nursery, so her daughter would have the right company. She had already learnt from the other parents that the day-care staff was diligent and qualified to take care of the kids. In addition, all parents would have access to a phone app, where they could live stream what was happening in the day care. Samara knew there would always be people who think differently from her, but she couldn't be bitter about it and change the course of her life to please them. She explained all these arrangements to her mother-in-law, who was supportive of her decision and also offered to stay with them for another three months in Bengaluru for additional help. Thus, through diligent planning and support of her family and organisation, Samara was able to fulfil her commitment of running her personal and professional lives in tandem.

My other conversation was with Seema, a vice president (VP) in the marketing team of a Mumbai-based conglomerate. Professionally she was a high achiever and had recently got a big promotion. She became pregnant soon after. On completing the first trimester of her pregnancy, Seema decided to put in her papers. When she mentioned this to me, I was surprised, since she had been doing quite well professionally. I asked her if she was feeling pressured by her husband, Samar, or her family to quit? Or did her organisation not have suitable policies for expectant mothers? In my mind, I was fairly sure that Seema hadn't thought through her decision. Otherwise, why would such a career-driven woman take this step? Instead, her reasoning educated me at some level and taught me not to be judgmental of career breaks. Seema had worked hard all her life. She was a top-ranking student throughout, and professionally too she had proved her mettle each year. Since this was her first pregnancy and she lived alone with her husband in Mumbai, she wanted to focus solely on herself and the baby growing inside her. She realised this was the time to take that well-earned break and work on her physical and mental well-being. She explained that while many people look at their careers like a sprint which has to be run in one go, she saw hers akin to a marathon, and she didn't feel insecure about taking a break during her run. She wanted to enjoy her pregnancy and the time with her baby. She had the confidence that she could rejoin work after some years when her baby was older. Till then, she was going to cherish this phase. Seema had also zeroed down on some online courses to study during her pregnancy which would help her upskill. She just wanted to use this time to learn and grow as a person.

After talking to Seema, I realised that we often approach life-changing decisions with apprehension and doubt, and in the process, we either spread ourselves too thin in an attempt to have it all or choose a single-focus road due to misgivings. I would say that no decision is wrong; it's the underlying motivation that differentiates a decision from a compulsion. For Seema, her decision was driven by the excitement of entering a new phase in her life that made her a happy woman and a happy mother in the making. Had the same decision been driven by social pressures or lack of family support, she would have felt disempowered and would have become bitter.

In order for a woman to balance her personal and professional lives, the assistance they must receive from their organisation is crucial. While many companies have the right plans to support their female employees, the intent does not always translate into actual action, leading to a huge gap between policies and their implementation. The next section of my book talks about the type of support professional women need within the workplace to continue with their careers uninterrupted, like their male counterparts. The book draws from my professional observations, interactions with women in the field and by studying the HR policies of various organisations on issues such as maternity, career progression, flexible working arrangements and mobility. The proposed guidelines are intended for companies to model the relevant policies in a way that lowers gender disparity while aiming for diversity and inclusion.

#RainmakerSpeak

Naiyya Saggi, founder and CEO, BabyChakra

Like me, Naiyya is a new mom. Her daughter and mine were born eight months apart. She became pregnant at a very crucial juncture of her professional life, when her start-up was ramping up towards a fundraise. I found Naiyya's approach to her pregnancy, motherhood and her work well thought out and practical. Her story, her ideas will help and motivate young mothers, who are juggling their professions alongside their journey of motherhood.

BabyChakra is a platform for pregnancy and childcare that attracts over a million unique visitors every month. It provides a personalised ecosystem for parents to connect with doctors, childcare experts and other parents for advice and discussion. Backed by several marquee funds and seasoned corporates, BabyChakra was part of the Google Accelerator Programme 2017 and was nominated by Google as one of the top seven innovative start-ups globally.

Naiyya Saggi, founder and CEO at BabyChakra, is a Harvard Business School alumna, where she was a Fulbright and J.N. Tata scholar. Before founding BabyChakra, she had considerable experience in maternity and childcare through her work at McKinsey& Company and at the Public Health Foundation of India. Naiyya is also a mentor at *#SheLeadsTech*, Facebook's flagship programme to support and accelerate Indian women founders in technology start-ups. Over the course of an interesting and informative chat, I learnt more about Naiyya and her start-up BabyChakra.

Tell us how you started on your journey with BabyChakra. What were your motivations and challenges in the process?
I have always wanted to create something impactful and help society with my work. The roots of this sentiment lie in my upbringing. Both my parents are government officials, devoted to the country's service; my mother is an IAS officer. After my schooling, I pursued law and then joined McKinsey, taking care of projects in the maternal and childcare space. It was here that I saw gaps in available information and guidance, but at that point, I wasn't sure about what I could do to make a difference.

Meanwhile, I got into Harvard Business School for my MBA, and my elder sister got pregnant during this time. She is a smart and confident corporate lawyer, but I could see how overwhelmed she was during her pregnancy. Being a first-time expectant mother, she would get unsolicited advice from everybody around her. In observing her situation came my eureka moment! I knew that I wanted to create a platform to help women in their journey through pregnancy and motherhood. This is how BabyChakra was built, based on the philosophy of being a non-judgmental companion to a mother in India while respecting her individuality.

During my journey of founding BabyChakra, I faced several biases. Some of them were quite explicit, like my experience during the angel round of funding where one of the investors asked me what would happen to the company if I became pregnant. I was shocked at such a sexist question, and it made me angry that I was being tested on my gender rather than my professional calibre. There were many instances of implicit bias too. In my initial years, oftentimes I felt I was being overlooked during networking events. Usually, venture capitalists have a stereotypical image of an entrepreneur in their mind—an IIT boy in a T-shirt and jeans, roaming around with a smart gadget. Who I was and how I looked didn't match this stereotype. But over the years, I have become tough-skinned and these things don't affect me as much. That said, this pattern-matching process does a great disservice to women and adds to their struggle of raising funds. But as we progress and see more women entrepreneurs, things will surely move towards equality.

Who has been your role model and what did you learn from them?

I credit my headstrong demeanour to my mother. She is a role model for both me and my sister. She has always had a very strong focus on education. My mother applied for the civil service exams when she was pregnant with my sister. Back then, she was in the city of Allahabad, where people would mock her for writing an exam during her pregnancy. But she showed great persistence and aced the exam to become an IAS officer. I have seen her handle difficult issues at her job, be it her interactions with the police, sorting out any strikes or helping maintain law and order.

Because of the strength my mother showcases, I have never thought of women as being the weaker sex. Like my mother, I would never compromise on my ambition and aspirations. Also, my parents had a marriage of equals and shouldered household responsibilities together. I would never play second fiddle in my career or in my marriage.

Do you see an economic benefit to gender inclusion, beyond it being the right thing to do?

The answer is a resounding yes! Globally, women comprise 51 per cent of traffic on digital platforms, but in India, the number stands at only 30 per cent. Women still borrow their husbands' smartphones in tier-3 and tier-4 cities because they lack access to data and electronic devices. This gap is closing rapidly. The future of digital expansion is women. With increasing numbers of women consumers, you need women at the table, conceptualising end-products or services for them.

I have experienced this first-hand. After becoming a mother, I became the end-user of my own platform, BabyChakra, and the quality of my insights into the products we sell got further refined. I could see a greater value-add to our business.

How do you ensure gender diversity at BabyChakra? Please share some initiatives close to your heart.

Unlike the general trend in India, we are a company with more women in the core team. At an organisational level, broadly 50 per cent of our workforce comprises women. We have always prioritised inclusion and a culture of openness, which is also visible in our policies. For instance, due to COVID-19, we announced a work-from-home plan almost a week before the nationwide lockdown was implemented. Our women employees were open with me and shared how overwhelmed they were in managing both home and office work. This is when we rolled out a policy of marking personal time-off (PTO) on calendars, during which employees can tend to their personal needs without being disturbed by office work. This helped in planning work better and kept the morale up too.

We also take mentoring our employees quite seriously. I am myself a part of mentor circles for women, such as Women in Tech and Women in Entrepreneurship, and because of this, a lot of hiring happens organically. For instance, our chief technical officer (CTO) is a woman who had been tracking my story. She reached out to me when there was a relevant opening and I knew that she would be a great fit. We get lucky that way in hiring and our company attracts the best of talents. When women see our high numbers of female leaders, they feel more comfortable in applying as they feel that BabyChakra will be a more inclusive workplace.

You got pregnant at a very crucial stage of your career, when you were planning to raise funds for your business. What were the main problems you faced?

My board and my employees were happy for me. They had full confidence in my capabilities and my commitment to BabyChakra. The story was a little different when it came to some of the investor meetings I went to. In a couple of fundraising conversations, I was politely advised to come back after my delivery. This is how typecasting and pigeonholing women manifests itself. There already exists a dearth of women entrepreneurs trying to begin new ventures and raising funds. To top that, I was a pregnant woman entrepreneur. I was an outlier who didn't fit the stereotypical pattern, and hence they were not comfortable dealing with me. But this didn't bother me as I had my team backing me up, and I had my eye on the goal which we successfully achieved.

Many women find it difficult to balance motherhood and career, and have to make tough choices along the way. How did you manage to find the equilibrium? Tell us about any initiatives in your organisation specifically targeted towards this issue.

I was cognizant of the fact that I will have to join back work very soon post-delivery. Therefore, I made arrangements accordingly. My mother-in-law moved in with us for the first four months to help my husband and me with the baby. My husband also supported me fully; he is a very involved father to our daughter. He realises that taking care of her is as much his responsibility as it is mine. And now we have a very trusted nanny to assist us.

For me, to be a happy mother, I need to be a happy person first. I cannot give the best to my child unless I am in a happy place mentally. I ignored all the naysayers who expected me to be a stay-at-home mom. I knew what was best for me and my daughter, and I acted accordingly.

At BabyChakra, we work hard to ensure that women on maternity leave don't feel neglected at work. Six months is a long time to be away, and often due to poor integration, once these new mothers are back at work, they feel lost and end up quitting, thereby dropping off the workforce. We proactively address this issue. For all managers, we have included 'proper integration of returning moms' as part of the critical performance indicator or KPI to ensure that everyone in the organisation takes it seriously. For instance, from the fifth month of the maternity break, short calls are scheduled with women on leave to help them mentally prepare for coming back to work. During these calls, we tell them what's happening in the company and in their teams. Once the employee joins back, the HR team assists and monitors them for the first thirty days to see that they are coping well emotionally. There are weekly catch-ups to address stress points, if any.

A lot of women are successful in different fields. How can they contribute towards inspiring the next generation?
It is critical to start with people in your own team first. Change begins with your immediate colleagues and then they, in turn, mentor women and men working for them. Let me share an incident here. A few years back, we had our first film shoot with CNBC Young Turks. For this, we had invited the community managers from our MomStar initiative. One of our MomStars,

a young woman with a small child, said that she couldn't come for the shoot because it was a working day and her husband wouldn't be available to look after the child. This is when I advised her to ask her husband to take a day's leave so that she could participate in the programme. Until I made the suggestion, it didn't even occur to her that this was an option. She did ask him and he agreed, so she was able to get her moment of glory by being a part of the programme.

Most women don't question the status quo, and I always encourage them to do that. Change will happen only when you take a step forward. However small you think that step may be, it will still lead you in the right direction.

Section II:

MAKING SENSE OF THE CORPORATE PLAYFIELD

7

Pro Tips for the Career Marathon

Whatever it is that you do in life, you need to be in the top three.

—Kalpana Morparia
Chairperson, South and South-East Asia, J.P. Morgan[1]

When I joined the banking industry in 2012, women's representation in the executive committees of major financial-services firms globally was less than 15 per cent (the number still stands at a low of 20 per cent).[2] Things haven't improved much even today, with India ranking third-lowest in the global representation of women managers and with only 2 per cent as CEOs;[3] we have very few women role models in the top echelons of the corporate world. In order to gain deeper insights into this field, I spoke with one of

[1] Designation as of 13 October 2020 when the interview was finalised.

[2] 'Oliver Wyman Women in Financial Services 2020' (https://www.oliverwyman.com/content/dam/oliver-wyman/v2/publications/2019/November/Women-In-Financial-Services-2020.pdf); Copyright (c) 2019 Oliver Wyman. All rights reserved.

[3] 'Women in Management'. Catalyst, 11 August 2020. Available at: https://www.catalyst.org/research/women-in-management/

the country's leading investment bankers, someone who symbolises the highest levels of determination, passion and perseverance.

#RainmakerSpeak

Kalpana Morparia, chairperson, South and South-East Asia, J.P. Morgan

I was lucky to have the opportunity of interacting with Kalpana Morparia, who helms J.P. Morgan, India. Kalpana has had a career spanning over 45 years, with exposure to both a domestic set-up (ICICI Bank) and a multinational ecosystem (J.P. Morgan). Starting her career in the 1970s, when it was extremely rare to see women in the world of finance and business, Kalpana has achieved the highest levels of corporate success, leading large organisations, holding multiple board positions and being credited with several industry recognitions along the way.

Kalpana rose to fame with her long innings at ICICI Bank, from where she retired in the year 2000, after 33 years of service. Prior to her retirement, Kalpana served as a joint managing director (MD) of the ICICI Group and vice-chair on the boards of the ICICI Group Companies. She played a pivotal role in establishing ICICI Bank as the largest private sector bank in India.

She joined J.P. Morgan as the CEO, India, in 2008, at a time when the global economy was being hit by the subprime crisis. After 12 years with the company, she is now the chairperson for J.P. Morgan, South and South-East Asia, and a member of J.P. Morgan's Asia-Pacific Management Committee.

Kalpana serves as an independent director on the boards of Dr. Reddy's Laboratories, Philip Morris International, Hindustan Unilever, and as a non-executive director on J.P. Morgan Services, India. She is also a member of the governing board of Bharti Foundation. She has been recognised, both internationally and in India, for being one of the leading women professionals in the world. Kalpana has also served on several committees constituted by the Government of India.[4]

Early days: The accidental banker

Kalpana grew up in a single-parent household, having lost her father when she was only six years old. Her guiding light was her mother, who pushed her very hard to focus on her studies. Kalpana's mother passionately believed that women require economic independence before marriage. Although her mother herself was not as well-educated, she knew the importance of education in shaping the career of her children.

Crazy as it may sound, this industry stalwart had no ambition of pursuing a corporate career. Kalpana wanted to marry early, right after completing school and have lots of children. In the course of her educational journey, this leading banker was never focused on the field of finance. Kalpana's mother aspired for her to be a doctor, so Kalpana took up science initially, but she did not study medicine. She completed her BSc in

[4] All official positions mentioned for Kalpana Morparia are as per the interview finalisation date, that is, 13 October 2020.

chemistry and microbiology, and took up a teaching job. Suffering a severe case of laryngitis, she had to take a break for 10 months, and during this time, out of boredom, she took to studying law. It was during this time that she married Jaisingh Morparia, who motivated her to complete her law degree and pursue a legal career. After completing her degree, Kalpana worked briefly at a law firm and then joined the legal department at ICICI Bank.

Kalpana's early journey is an interesting story of the right guidance she received during her childhood, the support she got to pursue her career choices and ultimately finding her true self.

Reflections from the past: Who is responsible for driving a meritocratic gender-inclusive work culture?

It was at ICICI Bank that Kalpana's journey of becoming a corporate leader started and, over a period of time, her personality underwent a sea change. Kalpana recalled that from the very beginning, she identified with the purpose of the organisation, which was to finance the industrialisation of India and to shape the banking industry. Being a self-driven individual, she was keen to contribute to this vision. As she progressed through her career, Kalpana identified four fundamental aspects that an organisation should have to drive a meritocratic gender-inclusive culture: visionary leadership, a supportive boss, a forward-thinking HR team and gender-inclusive company policies.

Support from the boss

During her formative years at ICICI, Kalpana believes her bosses had a critical role to play in providing the right fillip to her career. Two things were clearly against her. First, her background as a lawyer in a financial services firm pitted against peers with engineering, accountancy or business management qualifications, and second, her own personal phobia of public speaking. She needed a bit of self-awareness and confidence to help overcome these fears, and that's where her bosses came in.

Kalpana remembered, 'It took my bosses to draw it out for me that my academic qualifications didn't matter; what was critical was my approach to work and how I complemented my team through my skill set. This helped me gain confidence and the same reflected in my work. Thereon, I didn't scare away from any new assignments.

'As a child, I was once reprimanded by my teacher in front of the whole class on fumbling my lines during the school assembly. I felt very humiliated and this led me to lose my confidence in public speaking. I had made up my mind that I would never attempt public speaking again. After three or four years at ICICI, one of my managers asked me to go to a training college and give a lecture on law to seasoned bankers. I was understandably nervous, but I hesitantly decided to give it a shot and it paid off really well. My manager received phenomenal feedback for my session.

'This one incident of positive reinforcement by my manager brought back confidence in my public speaking skills and helped me better myself as a professional. So much so that I eventually became the official spokesperson for ICICI and a regular speaker at different forums. Looking back at it, I feel that I was lucky to have bosses who drew out my improvement areas and gave me an opportunity to work on them.'

These instances helped Kalpana realise the importance of working on her limitations, which has always helped in her career pursuits.

'I feel that tabling your limitations upfront is a great way to manage the expectations of the stakeholders, and it forces you to build complementary skills. The fact that I felt that finance was not my strong suit, but law, regulation and communication were, enabled me when my boss gave me some tough assignments. I identified my inadequacies myself and shared themselves with my boss, who ensured that I got the freedom to pick people who complemented my skill set. Therefore, together we were a winning team,' she explained.

As a word of advice for bosses and reporting managers, Kalpana said, 'Each one of us has some perceived limitations in our mind, and if a good boss or a good senior colleague draws that out, one can snap out of that perceived weakness quickly.'

A forward-thinking HR team

Kalpana's formative years at a gender-neutral organisation like ICICI moulded her personality and gave her opportunities to grow and progress. This experience made her falsely believe that women in all organisations enjoyed similar equality. Naturally, when she joined J.P. Morgan, she came with the same mindset that assumed that women thrive on their merit and equal opportunities. During our interaction, Kalpana recalled the turning point that changed her approach to gender inclusion:

'At J.P. Morgan, as a senior leader, I would be requested to speak at networking events for women. Often at these events, I would ask the audience, why were we there at all? After all, women didn't need any special help to excel and move forward in their profession.

'After one such event, my HR head, who was a man, told me, "You know what you have just ended up doing? You have ensured that no woman raises her hand to tell you if she has a gender-related problem or concern to share." This was a wake-up call for me! It meant that I needed to have an open mind and become sensitive to the broader canvas that existed.'

Kalpana acknowledges that without the transparency in the system, which enabled her head of HR to pinpoint the flaw in her thinking, her awareness of gender-related issues at the workplace would remain limited.

Gender-inclusive company policies

Kalpana feels strongly about the vital role an organisation and its policies can play in supporting and retaining women, especially during times of personal milestones when women need additional support. In 45 years of her experience, Kalpana said, she has seen many women who chose to drop off their career path, burdened by additional responsibilities that come with having a child. A few amongst these women were comfortable with the choice they made, but a vast majority of them were not happy with it. This is because their decision was made due to social constraints, not having a supportive spouse or family, or lacking support from their organisation, which made them feel irrelevant during their maternity leave. Kalpana stressed the fact that society as a whole, and companies in particular, should work towards creating a suitable support system so that women don't feel pressured to make such choices.

'Most organisations have 40 to 50 per cent women employees at the entry-level, particularly in the services sector. But then you see this huge leakage at the mid-level which of course leads to a paucity of women in senior and leadership roles. So, organisations need to ask themselves how they can support women during this phase so that they don't feel alienated when they go on a maternity break.

'Let me cite a personal example here from when one of my lead research analysts went on a maternity break. While she took leave to spend time with her baby, she continued to be in touch with the team and even wrote some reports during this time. So, that link between the organisation and her never broke off. This made her maternity leave comfortable and she could return full-time to work without feeling disconnected with her team and the company.'

Beyond awareness and sensitivity to specific milestones, Kalpana is a strong proponent of implementing and enabling policies to enhance overall opportunities for women in the organisation. At J.P. Morgan, she is proud of several initiatives made by the firm, including networking events and general awareness on gender inclusion, among others.

'I see great merit in organising networking events for women. At the end of a working day, most women rush home to attend to household responsibilities. They don't do much voluntary networking post-work-hours, while men do this quite naturally. So, when you create an official networking event, women feel obligated to attend it, and in doing so, they interact with so many people—senior management, leaders, clients, colleagues from different departments—and in all these interactions they get to learn so much, they get exposed to so much. This opens new opportunities for them and it's a super support system. We at J.P. Morgan call these events 'Women on the Move', and we invite not only women but a lot of men too and create a safe space for women to discuss their issues. We also do networking events with our women clients and try to get into the broader community.

'Companies should change some of their policies and processes, become more sensitive to gender bias and how it can play out in their decision-making while hiring, doing evaluations and giving promotions. For instance, during International Women's Week, we organised a role-based learning session on gender biases, where a group enacted what may unknowingly happen in a typical family where they prefer a male child over a female one. When such role plays happen, people tend to absorb the key message and bring a change in both their personal and professional lives.

'Another enabling policy at J.P. Morgan which I would like to highlight is the Manager-Connect policy, under which we ensure proper integration of women on sabbatical or maternity leave so that the organisation, their manager and their teams don't lose touch with the employees on a break. We seek to retain all of them when they return from their leave. We work a lot with college campuses as well and do dedicated interactions with women candidates, highlighting what a career with J.P. Morgan offers them.'

The role of a visionary leadership

Kalpana believes that the top leadership plays a pivotal role in pushing a gender-inclusive structure in any organisation. She mentions that at J.P. Morgan, diversity and inclusion are important agenda points that are practised globally and are much broader in their implementation. In each region, the focus is on issues that are socially relevant to that particular place. For instance, in the US, you may see an equal emphasis on race, while in India, the focus is on gender issues since we see fewer women representatives at senior levels. Any significant focus on gender inclusion by the leadership will flow down to the rest of the organisation. Apart from the leadership's vision, Kalpana also stressed the need for tracking performances on objective metrics, without biases, to ensure accountability.

Given Kalpana's rich experience and responsibilities of managing multiple geographies, I asked her how

India fares when it comes to gender inclusion in the workplace.

'We focus a lot on tracking gender metrics in India. While ensuring a healthy diversity slate when we seek job applicants, we track how many women we finally hire. We also look at attrition closely and keep a close check on gender ratio across management levels and departments.

'I also stress immensely on implementing policies that would support improving the gender ratio in the company, and organise bias-sensitisation training to educate all employees so they can minimise any unfairness which may crop up in their day to day working.'

My interaction with Kalpana brought forth many aspects of the Power Punch framework, which will form the core of the second segment of the book, the most important being the role of corporate influencers in enabling a woman's career based on her capability, without focusing on her gender. This interaction laid the right foundation for the next section of the book, which builds a case towards having more women in the corporate world, especially at the leadership levels. It also focuses on the role played by various stakeholders in ensuring gender inclusion (detailed in the Power Punch framework).

8

The Business Case for Women

A diverse workforce is essential to our success as a multi-national, multi-cultural business.

—Diageo, a global leader in beverage alcohol, on diversity[1]

As a leading producer of spirits in the world and operating in more than 180 countries, Diageo not only believes in the above statement, but also implements it closely within the organisation. Women occupy 39 per cent of leadership roles in the company; they constitute 50 per cent of Diageo's board and 38 per cent of their executive committee.[2] Diageo continues to occupy top positions in global diversity-and-inclusion indices. In 2019, they were ranked second in the Refinitiv (formerly Thomson Reuters) Global Diversity and Inclusion Index and named number one globally for gender equality by gender analysis company Equileap. They have also been recognised by Bloomberg's Gender-Equality Index (GEI). Diageo acknowledges the merits of gender inclusion and is aiming to have 40 per cent women in the senior leadership team by 2025.

[1] https://www.diageo.com/en/in-society/doing-business-the-right-way/investing-in-our-people/

[2] https://www.diageo.com/en/in-society/building-thriving-communities/investing-in-our-people/

Building a diverse workforce and an inclusive culture can prove to be a value-accretive practice for any organisation as it drives better business performance, augments its brand value and keeps employees happy.

The first step towards building an inclusive corporate ecosystem is to make organisations understand that gender inclusion is not just a social agenda but a business imperative that accrues tangible benefits to an organisation. To the credit of the corporate world, gender equality is finally being looked at as an important criterion to meet. According to the 2017 PwC Annual Survey, 87 per cent of CEOs across the globe said they were focused on talent diversity and inclusiveness to drive greater innovation and create competitive advantage.[3] This is a welcome sign for the business world.

When more than 70 per cent of consumer purchasing decisions are made by women,[4] doesn't it make sense for more women to be present at each level in the corporate value chain since they understand the needs of their own demographic better?

Let us delve into the specific impact that gender balance can create for organisations, summing up the business case for having women across the chain of any organisation. There are three main areas where gender inclusion creates a positive impact, as highlighted in

[3] 'Winning the Fight for Female Talent' (https://www.pwc.com/gx/en/about/diversity/iwd/iwd-female-talent-report-web.pdf); Copyright (c) 2017 PwC. All rights reserved. Sourced with permission.

[4] https://www.forbes.com/sites/forbescontentmarketing/2019/05/13/20-facts-and-figures-to-know-when-marketing-to-women/#6b55537f1297

the following chart: financial impact, impact on brand value and human impact (talent and cultural).

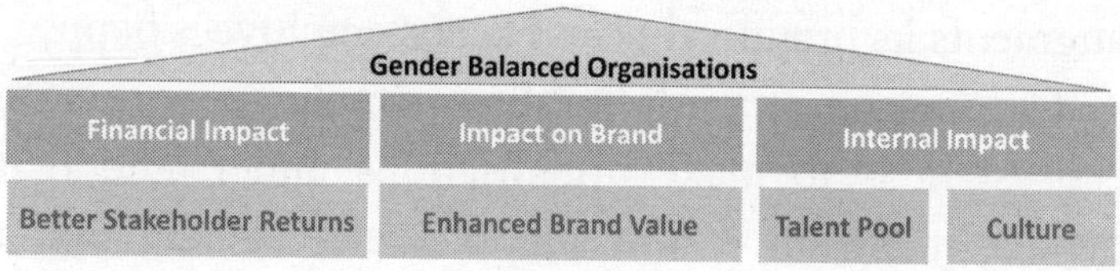

Financial impact

Promoting gender parity is smart economics for any organisation. Sodexo's gender-balance study bears proof of their improved performance by gender-balanced teams. In 2018, Sodexo conducted an extensive survey involving 50,000 managers across 70 business entities worldwide and found that performance improved with a 40 to 60 per cent female workforce.[5] With the gender balance in this zone, the teams scored better on five business parameters[6]:

- Operating margins—eight percentage points higher
- Client retention—nine percentage points higher
- Employee retention—eight percentage points higher
- Employee engagement—fourteen percentage points higher
- Safety (decreased workplace accident rates)—twelve percentage points higher

Sodexo leads by example and has already made notable progress on gender inclusion—women constitute 35

[5] 'Sodexo's Gender Balance Study 2018'; Copyright (c) 2018 Sodexo Operations, LLC. Sourced with permission.

[6] Ibid.

per cent of its executive committee and 60 per cent of its board of directors.[7] Sodexo's CEO has committed to reach a global representation of 40 per cent women in senior leadership by 2025.[8] Additionally, Sodexo has a target that all employees work for gender-balanced management teams by 2025.[9]

A McKinsey study, 'Diversity Wins', published in 2020, also backs up the positive financial impact of having women in leadership roles. It states that companies in the top-quartile for gender diversity on executive teams were 25 per cent more likely to outperform on profitability (up from 21 per cent in 2017).[10] In fact, organisations with more than 30 per cent women in their executive teams are significantly more likely to outperform those with fewer women. The substantial performance differential between the most and least gender-diverse companies can be as high as 48 per cent.[11]

Another related study by McKinsey published in 2018, 'Delivering through Diversity', had Sodexo as part of the study, and it was voted among the most gender-diverse companies in its industry group and home country. It was also among the most successful company financially,

[7] https://www.globenewswire.com/news-release/2020/07/02/2056946/0/en/Sodexo-ranked-2-for-gender-balance-within-its-governing-bodies-among-2019-French-publicly-listed-companies.html

[8] 'Sodexo's Gender Balance Study 2018'; Copyright (c) 2018 Sodexo Operations, LLC. Sourced with permission.

[9] Ibid.

[10] Based on the data gathered in 2019. 'Diversity wins: How inclusion matters', May 2020, McKinsey & Company, www.mckinsey.com; Copyright (c) 2021 McKinsey & Company. All rights reserved. Reprinted by permission.

[11] Ibid.

within McKinsey's dataset, with value creation of 13 per cent above the industry average.[12]

Studies such as these are often questioned and it is maintained that there are several departments and roles that are male-dominated for a reason and shouldn't be changed. This argument is quelled by Lizzie Chapman, co-founder and CEO of ZestMoney. Typically, the collection departments of lending companies are male-dominated, with stereotypical images of aggressive, loud people. ZestMoney, however, works differently. Their collection team comprises 60 per cent women, and most of the employees in this team have a customer services background. This has led to ZestMoney achieving a high collection rate and fewer delinquencies, compared to its competitors.

It is indeed time that businesses all around the world take into account the financial impact of having a diverse workforce across the corporate hierarchy and start laying down an action-oriented roadmap to achieve the same. While things may be working just fine, can they improve further with a more balanced workforce? Organisations like Sodexo, ZestMoney and many others definitely think so!

Brand impact

Adopting a value system internally and externally lets organisations connect with all stakeholders, including

[12] 'Delivering through diversity', January 2018, McKinsey & Company, www.mckinsey.com;

customers, employees and business partners, thereby augmenting the company's brand value.

More than ever, we must be exemplary and stand for inclusion in the workplace, supporting the social and economic progress of the communities in which we operate. We remain fully committed and maintain our comprehensive initiatives and collective efforts towards gender-balance at all levels of our company.
—Cathy Desquesses, chief people officer, Sodexo[13]

In 2019, Sodexo was ranked second among French publicly listed companies for gender balance within its governing bodies. Such industry accolades and recognition for Sodexo for its work on gender equality adds to its brand value. Customers and business partners today are cognizant of a business's role as a corporate citizen and its contribution towards driving social change. Gender parity and inclusion are areas where organisations can work directly and show tangible progress.

Companies with a strong focus on driving a positive change in society through their brand gather immense respect and recognition. It helps them connect with consumers with agendas that are important to them. Let's take P&G as another example and look at how it propagates equality and sustainability through its brands. The advertising campaigns for some of its marquee brands are always in pursuit of a

[13] https://www.globenewswire.com/news-release/2020/07/02/2056946/0/en/Sodexo-ranked-2-for-gender-balance-within-its-governing-bodies-among-2019-French-publicly-listed-companies.html

positive change in society, thereby resonating well with its customers. The company has adopted a set of frameworks called Brand 2030. One of the brand fundamentals focuses on P&G leveraging the voice of its brands in communication and advertising production to promote social and environmental sustainability.[14]

For instance, through its brand Ariel, P&G is challenging the social expectation of household chores being disproportionately done by women. With its *#ShareTheLoad* campaign, it is raising a pertinent question about the way we raise our sons and the need to teach them what we teach our daughters. A popular advert from the *#ShareTheLoad* series shows the following.

A father visiting his married daughter notices that when she returns home from work, she dives straight into household chores—helping her son with homework, cooking dinner, offering her husband evening tea, putting the laundry in the washing machine—alongside returning some office emails and calls. He feels proud yet disappointed to see his daughter seamlessly managing office work and housework. He starts introspecting about how his daughter would have learnt this over-burdened multitasking by observing him and her mother. After all, he too never helped his wife in any household chores. Similarly, his son-in-law would have grown up in a family where the wife alone would take care of household chores while the

[14] https://assets.ctfassets.net/oggad6svuzkv/c5IrnXxwqeuG0x4RUPJ4o/daef678c940da189cdacc0a7723e5ee7/P_G-Ambition2030-Brands-Final_4.8.19v2.pdf

husband would be busy reading the newspaper and drinking tea. The girl's father, on returning home to his wife, leaves behind a letter for his daughter where he apologises for this gendered upbringing. He accepts that he has been setting the wrong example through his conduct so far, but he is now going to correct this behaviour by being a better husband to his wife… beginning with helping her with the laundry. He hopes that each small step towards building a more equal marriage will set the right example for future generations.

#ShareTheLoad has won P&G tremendous respect and love from its customers. The brilliance of the concept and the change it was trying to bring about were recognised both nationally and internationally through numerous awards. It won five Cannes Lions[15] in 2016, making Ariel India the most awarded Indian campaign in the event's history. It also won other awards, including the coveted Laadli Grand Prix Award, Gold Emvies and Black Dragon at Dragons of Asia.

Beyond maintaining inclusion among employees and propagating it in society through its brands, P&G also strives towards gender equality in its channel partners. For instance, it expects gender-equal teams from its advertising agencies. By 2023, the company wants women film directors for half of its product

[15] Started in 1954, Cannes Lions International Festival of Creativity has been bringing the creative communications industry together every year at its one-of-a-kind event in Cannes to learn, network and celebrate.

commercials.[16] It's also committed to expanding its supplier base to women-owned businesses across the world, including the Indian subcontinent.[17] Thus, P&G's philosophy on diversity is very well-rounded and holistic as reflected in the statement below:

> ...diversity is essential in all we do, we believe inclusion changes the game. Every day we strive to get the full value of our diversity through inclusion—fostering an environment where P&G people can be their best, full and authentic selves in the workplace.[18]

These initiatives have made P&G the voice of change, with a high brand value and brand recall, both internally for its employees and externally for all other stakeholders including its customers, business partners and shareholders.

While we have talked about the positives, companies that have been lax about bringing in and implementing gender-balanced systems have faced some serious repercussions. For instance, some companies lost millions in market value as an aftermath of the *#MeToo* allegations. Customers and business partners tend to disassociate themselves from brands with a less-than-satisfactory stand on gender issues. Goldman Sachs,

[16] https://economictimes.indiatimes.com/magazines/panache/an-equal-pitch-by-2023-pg-wants-half-of-its-commercials-to-be-made-by-women/articleshow/64635064.cms?from=mdr

[17] https://brandequity.economictimes.indiatimes.com/news/marketing/pg-makes-a-new-move-to-support-gender-equality/57092136

[18] 'P&G 2019 Citizenship Report'; Copyright (c) 2019 Procter & Gamble. Sourced with permission.

one of the largest investment banks in the world, announced that it would not do IPOs for companies with an all-male board. The CEO, David Solomon, had this to say:

> Effective July 1 [2020], Goldman Sachs will only underwrite IPOs in the US and Europe of private companies that have at least one diverse board member. And starting in 2021, we will raise this target to two diverse candidates for each of our IPO clients.
>
> This decision is rooted first and foremost in our conviction that companies with diverse leadership perform better. Consider this: since 2016, US companies that have gone public with at least one female board director outperformed companies that do not, one year post-IPO.[19]

Internal impact on the talent pool and work culture

Talent plays a central role in the growth and success of an organisation. Unless the employees are happy and committed to performing to their best of capabilities, the organisation will not be able to flourish. It is not uncommon to see many CEOs crediting the organisation's success to the hard work of its workforce. The common theme emerging from these successful companies is that a diverse workforce backed by an inclusive culture strives to perform their best. It has been observed that diverse teams are better

[19] https://www.goldmansachs.com/our-commitments/diversity-and-inclusion/launch-with-gs/pages/commitment-to-diversity.html

at innovation and creative solutions. When different people with unique perspectives come together, it leads to holistic discussions and better decision-making, driven by higher creativity. This may be the reason behind the outperformance of gender-diverse organisations, compared to their peers. As Rohini Anand, PhD, former senior VP and global chief diversity officer, Sodexo, says, 'A balanced talent-mix, combined with an inclusive culture helps to enhance innovation, engagement and productivity to achieve the right business outcomes.'[20]

In addition to a motivated workforce that bolsters the performance of a company, diverse organisations also enjoy the benefits of lower recruitment cost and find it much easier to attract top-notch talent. In a world where recruitment can cost millions and takes up considerable time, this is a great advantage. Reflecting back on my interaction with Lizzie, we see how ZestMoney has achieved equal representation with an almost 50:50 gender ratio at the organisational level. At the C-suite level, they have 60 per cent women. This has made hiring talented people easier and less time-consuming for them. They get to choose from among the most qualified and experienced women candidates, and the common feedback they get from all these candidates is that they feel it is a fair place where they can make a career for life by looking at the diverse workforce.

When a company gets to choose from the finest within a talent pool, they have the best people for each role. These organisations also tend to report lower

[20] 'Sodexo's Gender Balance Study 2018'; Copyright (c) 2018 Sodexo Operations, LLC. Sourced with permission.

attrition levels, owing to higher work satisfaction among employees. As a starting point, it creates a safe and healthy working environment, where employees feel more comfortable sharing their views because they see themselves represented by others in the organisation. Salesforce, for instance, went a step ahead and created a new C-suite position in 2016, the 'chief equality officer'. Chair, CEO and founder Marc Benioff mentioned in one of his interviews that at Salesforce, equality is job one and thus it needs a senior executive running it. Reporting directly to Marc, the chief equality officer Tony Prophet is responsible for building an inclusive workplace that reflects the diverse communities Salesforce serves and further the cause of equality for all.[21] In the same vein, Richard Branson says, 'Clients do not come first. Employees come first. If you take care of your employees, they will take care of the clients.'

Organisations taking the inclusion mandate seriously need to propagate the business case for it. When all stakeholders—the top leadership, heads of business, employees—see the economic value of gender inclusion, they will start approaching it like an important business driver, with a defined roadmap and accountability to achieve it.

Currently, at many organisations, the responsibility of gender inclusion lies with the HR team. To the credit of the HR community, they have done a fair bit, but unless the idea percolates to all stakeholders, the march

[21] https://www.salesforce.com/company/leadership/bios/bio-prophet/

towards achieving true gender balance will continue to be an uphill task. Enabling policies are present in most organisations, but there is a lack of true implementation and support by the system.

To bring about a sustainable wave of change, there is a need to educate people on the business benefits of gender inclusion and track it as an accountable metric across the organisation. Everyone has a role to play in this process, and the Power Punch framework summarises the same.

#InclusionStalwart

Procter & Gamble

In fact, one of the reasons why I believe we're delivering stronger results is because we've activated the full capability of P&G people—a key tenet of our Diversity & Inclusion work. A diverse team with an inclusive environment that values every individual will outperform a homogeneous team, and that's what the 97,000 employees of P&G are demonstrating.

—David S. Taylor

Chairman of the board, president and CEO, P&G[22]

P&G, the glorious 180-year-old consumer conglomerate, has been actively championing gender equality both internally and externally. It is among those organisations that are very clear on the areas they can have an impact and then relentlessly work in those

[22] 'P&G 2019 Citizenship Report'; Copyright (c) 2019 Procter & Gamble. Sourced with permission.

streams with commitment and a data-driven approach. The gender equality efforts of P&G are focused on three areas where they feel that they can have the greatest impact:

- Leveraging their significant voice in advertising and media to tackle gender bias through campaigns like Ariel's *#ShareTheLoad*, Secret deodorant's *#AllStrengthNoSweat*, Always's *#LikeAGirl* and the Always Saudi's *#WeAreTheGenerationOfFirsts*.
- Removing gender-biased barriers to education for girls and providing economic opportunities for women through their corporate programmes and policy advocacy efforts.
- Creating an inclusive, gender-equal environment inside P&G, and advocating for gender-equal workplaces beyond P&G, where everyone can contribute to their full potential.[23]

Don't these numbers speak for themselves?

P&G's global workforce representation by gender is a testimony to the fact that they have found the secret sauce to enable gender equality and inclusion. An increase from 26 per cent women in 2015 to 41 per cent women in 2020 in the Global Leadership Council is commendable and shows that P&G is moving in the right direction towards building a gender equal working ecosystem.

[23] 'P&G Citizenship Report 2020'; Copyright (c) 2019 Procter & Gamble. Sourced with permission.

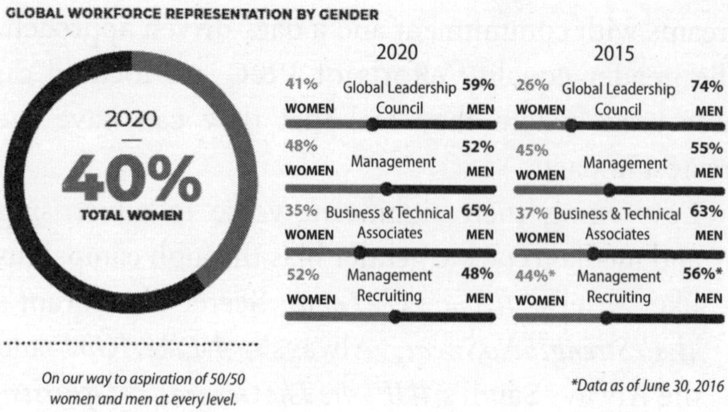

[24]

Gender equality and inclusion is not only for employees

Citizenship cannot be something done on the side; it has to be built into how we do business every day.

—David S. Taylor

Chairman of the board, president and CEO, P&G[25]

The internal commitment to diversity and inclusion reflects in the way P&G conducts its day-to-day business. Through their brands, they use their voice on important issues such as gender inclusion, racial equality and pay equality. Their campaigns such as *#ShareTheLoad*, *#WeSeeEqual* and *#LikeAGirl* encourage important conversations in the societies in which P&G operates.

As a consumer, a woman, a wife and a mother, I must say that these acts of corporate citizenship by P&G

[24] 'P&G Citizenship Report 2020'; Copyright (c) 2019 Procter & Gamble. Sourced with permission.

[25] Ibid.

draw me closer to its brands and make me happy to see the kind of change they are enabling in the world. Talking specifically about India, an independent survey indicates that over the last five years, Ariel has positively influenced men to share the load. From 79 per cent men in 2014 who thought doing the laundry was only a woman's job, the number has steadily declined to 41 per cent in 2019.[26] Such has been the power of P&G's gender-sensitive advertising. Another brand I would like to mention here is Whisper, which stands out with its campaigns like *#TouchThePickle*, *#SitImproper* and *#WhispersBreakSilence*. Through these campaigns, Whisper has been leveraging its voice to remove society's taboo towards menstruation. Their latest campaign *#KeepGirlsInSchool* focuses on preventing girls from dropping out of schools because of puberty. Whisper has pledged to double the impact of its menstrual hygiene education programme by reaching five crore adolescent girls by 2022.[27]

My key takeaway from observing P&G remains how it is congruent in its value system internally and externally. I believe this holistic approach towards corporate citizenship has established P&G as a powerhouse brand to reckon with in the eyes of all its stakeholders—employees, consumers, suppliers and channel partners. P&G's success as a global organisation adds merit to the case for working towards building a diverse and inclusive organisation.

[26] 'P&G India Citizenship Report 2020'; Copyright (c) 2019 Procter & Gamble. Sourced with permission.

[27] Ibid.

9

The Power Punch

India's employment survey shows that among women in the prime working ages of 30 to 50 years, more than two-thirds are not in the workforce, with the majority of them reporting that they are attending to only domestic duties.[1]

The education statistics for women have bettered over the years in our country, but their financial independence remains a concern as evident from the statistics from India's employment survey. If we talk about India's female labour force participation rate—calculated as the share of women who are employed or are seeking work as a proportion of the working-age female population—it stands distressingly low at 23.4 per cent (2019) as per the World Bank (modelled ILO estimates).[2] Compared to neighbouring nations like Bhutan (58.3 per cent), Nepal (81.6 per cent),

[1] https://www.livemint.com/news/india/india-s-workforce-is-masculinising-rapidly-1560150389726.html

[2] https://www.telegraphindia.com/opinion/economic-survey-2020-60-per-cent-of-women-in-india-in-the-productive-age-bracket-of-15-59-years-are-engaged-in-full-time-housework/cid/1762953

China (60.63 per cent), Bangladesh (36.14 per cent), Myanmar (47.54 per cent) and Sri Lanka (34.75 per cent), this doesn't paint a very good picture.[3] For the urban woman too, the statistics are not encouraging. It isn't a surprise to see that only 3.7 per cent of CEOs and MDs of NSE-listed companies were women in 2019, a number that has increased just slightly from 3.2 per cent in 2014.[4] What did come as a surprise, however, was that the HR field, which is looked at as woman-dominated turf in India, also had only 31 per cent women occupying the CHRO role (chief human resources officer), a role which is overrepresented by women in other countries such as the US and South Africa.[5] The cherry on the cake is that, as of 2019, just 29 companies (5.8 per cent) on the Fortune India 500 list had women in executive roles.[6] Numbers in 2021 are not off to a great start either with only one woman as the CEO in the coveted Nifty 50 companies and only five holding the position at the top 100 largest companies in India.[7]

The reason why we have such under-representation of women at senior levels is the already thin and further dwindling talent pipeline of women across levels. Many

[3] https://www.telegraphindia.com/opinion/economic-survey-2020-60-per-cent-of-women-in-india-in-the-productive-age-bracket-of-15-59-years-are-engaged-in-full-time-housework/cid/1762953

[4] 'Women in the Workforce: India'. Catalyst, 28 October 2020. Available at: https://www.catalyst.org/research/women-in-the-workforce-india/

[5] Ibid.

[6] Ibid.

[7] https://insideiim.com/women-ceo-fortune-500-companies

women enter the workforce but see a high attrition rate around mid-management levels.[8]

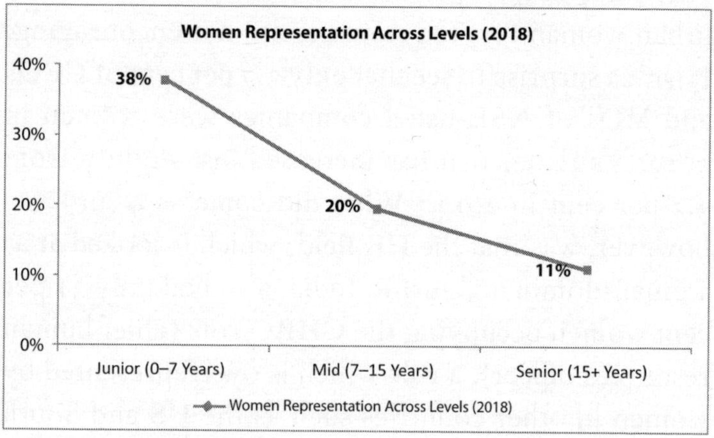

It comes as no surprise that this stage coincides with women experiencing an increase in their domestic responsibilities after marriage and motherhood. While we assume that women make an independent choice to focus more on their family and raise kids in this phase, we never question why a woman who has been as ambitious as her male colleagues thus far has to make such a choice. What is corporate India missing?

Let's start by looking at a case study.

Organisation A takes pride in its approach to women employees. It has recently launched new policies on flexi-hours, work from home and an unpaid sabbatical of three to six months in addition to maternity leave.

[8] According to a study a management consulting firm, Zinnov, in collaboration with Intel India (https://www.livemint.com/news/india/women-s-representation-inindian-companies-rises-11576086142768.html).

The HR department and the CEO of the company are thoroughly satisfied and laud themselves on the launch of these policies.

Now, let's cut to the grass-roots realities. Arya is a 35-year-old mid-management VP in the organisation. She has an MBA with impeccable academic credentials; she has over eight years of prior work experience, which is very rich and relevant to her current role.

Arya has been with the organisation for three years now. She has been a high achiever, taking the initiative in projects, and is smarter than the average lot in the company. In this time span, she is already leading important projects for the firm. She is now up for a promotion in the current appraisal cycle. The appraisals are set to begin in May.

On the personal front, Arya and her husband have been trying for a baby for a few months. In April, to their immense happiness, they find out that they are expecting and are ecstatic and nervous like any other first-time parents. During a visit to their gynaecologist for a check-up, Arya is recommended two weeks of rest. Since the pregnancy is in its early stages, she decides to keep the news limited to her immediate family.

At the office, Arya has been working on a very important strategic project for close to six months that is now at its final stages and heading towards closure. All the heavy-lifting on the project is already done and all that remains are some closure meetings with senior people. Since Arya has been closely working with the MD on this project, she calls him on a Saturday morning and tells him that due to a cervical spondylosis issue, she has to work from home for two weeks. The MD is supportive on the call. Arya feels relieved.

In these two weeks, while taking adequate rest and working from home, Arya continues to be at the top of her game, workwise. She manages to go to the office for important meetings and closes all work streams on the project well in time.

By the time Arya returns to work, the appraisals have already started. The day of her review meeting comes by. The MD and the reporting manager, a senior VP with the firm, sit in her review. They praise and recognise all the hard work she has been putting into the project and the tangible value addition that she has done to build a strong brand for the organisation.

They then move forward to discuss her development areas, which Arya expects to be related to skill enhancement, so she can further grow as a professional. To her utter surprise, the MD instead asks about her health and if she falls sick often. Arya is taken aback since apart from the recent break, she has seldom taken a sick leave in three years! Never the one to mince words, Arya clarifies her position. Then some more feedback comes Arya's way, advising her to network more within the organisation, which seems unjustified to her, given that the kind of projects Arya has led have made her interact with people across the length and breadth of the organisation. When Arya highlights this, the MD feigns surprise, adding that he was giving friendly advice since women, in general, find it tough to network.

Arya is deeply disappointed after the review, reflecting on how her hard work in the last few months was downplayed and disregarded. She is subjected to intangible criticism, without any reference to her actual performance and track record. In response, Arya's manager emphasises that the firm was cooperative in allowing her to work from home. Reminding them of the recently launched work-from-home policies, Arya assertively mentions that despite working from home, all her work commitments were delivered well in time, and she was in the office to close all the meetings. Arya found appalling the gaping difference between the written policy and its implementation.

That day, Arya goes back home a little dejected with the system and its hypocrisy. Later that night, she reflects on the events and conversations of the past few days. She knows she has some important decisions to make.

What happened in the case of Arya? Who was accountable here? Was it the leadership? The HR team or the reporting manager? In theory, what comes across as a great organisation, with forward-thinking policies and guidelines on paper, may turn out to be lacking when it comes to implementing the same policies.

How can women navigate these situations better? Is there something organisations can do to avoid such circumstances?

Imagine a boxing match where you have to deliver the perfect punch to win, and it's not just one punch, it's a series of perfect punches. For this, you need to form a solid fist with your five fingers, backed by your boxing skills and winning spirit. Similarly, for an equitable and inclusive corporate playfield, there are five influencers who need to be in complete sync with the corporate ethos to generate the maximum economic benefit for an organisation. I call it the Power Punch:

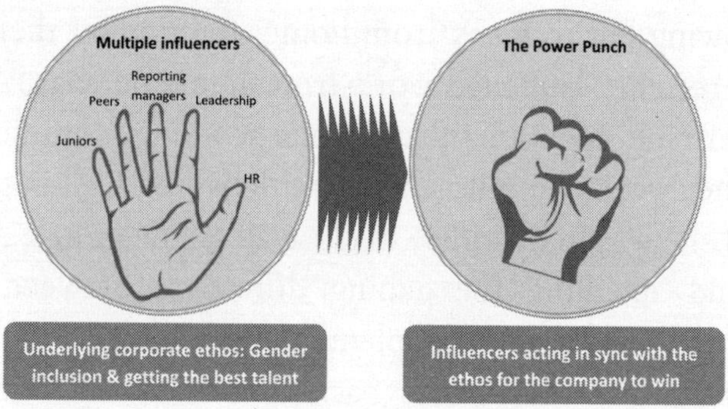

As we progress through the chapters, I explain how each of these influencers plays an important role in any employee's work life. Unless these influencers operate with a gender-neutral approach, the organisation will not be able to reap the maximum benefits from the talent it houses. This is exactly how we ensure a strong fist for that perfect punch where, just like our corporate influencers, each finger is equally important and has its own unique role and position in delivering the maximum impact.

#RainmakerSpeak

Lizzie Chapman, co-founder and CEO, ZestMoney

No company better demonstrates how different corporate influencers work seamlessly to create a gender-agnostic work culture than fintech start-up ZestMoney. Both technology and finance are male-dominated fields, and ZestMoney, with the majority of the founders being women, brings in a whiff of fresh air. Today, it has become the largest and fastest-growing consumer-lending fintech company in India. It was founded in 2015 by CEO Lizzie Chapman, CFO/COO Priya Sharma and CTO Ashish Anantharaman, who were all colleagues at Wonga, a UK-based finance company. ZestMoney is backed by several marquee funds and leading global digital financial services investors.

Lizzie is a prominent figure in the digital lending ecosystem of India. She is a British national who started her career in the world of finance and investments with Goldman Sachs in London. In 2011, she moved to India to set up the Indian operations of Wonga. Two years later, she joined DBS to lead the launch of Digibank, a mobile-only virtual bank. In 2015, she took the plunge of co-founding ZestMoney with Priya and Ashish. Today these three professionals have led ZestMoney to great heights. The company's innovative technology and work, to make affordable digital finance accessible widely, led to their selection as the World Economic Forum's Technology Pioneers of 2020.[9]

Lizzie is recognised as one of India's top 100 women in finance and has been honoured with numerous accolades for her work in the field of fintech. She received the Female Fintech Leader award in 2017 and the Women in Fintech award in 2019. As a mother of one, she strikes a happy balance between her work and family life. Through her conduct and working style, Lizzie leads by example to show how to accomplish being a woman in business and a working mother at the same time. She is a role model for scores of women,

[9] https://www.zestmoney.in/about-us/

both inside and outside ZestMoney. Over a long chat, I asked her about her journey in the process of setting up her own firm in India.

How did you begin your journey with ZestMoney and what were the main challenges you faced?
The start-up sector is male-dominated all over the world. In fact, I had more sexist encounters in Europe, where discrimination against women in the world of finance is more prevalent than in India. The prejudice in the UK was more blatant and obvious. The policies and guidelines were top-notch, but the day-to-day work environment was insensitive. In India, I found things to be much better, since I didn't feel the need to ape men to succeed. But let me give a disclaimer here—I was an outsider, a foreigner working in India, so maybe people behaved differently with me compared to my co-founder Priya, who is an Indian.

During our fundraising phase, one of our global investors voiced their concern regarding hiring men in a start-up with more women heading the business than men. I was glad that these apprehensions were being discussed upfront, as it avoids blind spots about such ethical issues later. Honestly, we didn't really face any issues in this regard, since Priya and I have managed hundreds of employees in the past, with the majority being men. Our third co-founder and CTO, Ashish, is a man who stands firmly with us in trying to establish the right work culture at ZestMoney. Given that we are three diverse professionals at the top level, we are able to maintain and percolate that diversity all the way down. We don't encourage any kind of 'boys' club' culture being formed within the company. It is only merit which drives all our decisions while hiring potential employees, and not based on whether one is socially compatible or not.

How does gender inclusion contribute to your organisational culture, its brand value and its income and profitability?
I can unhesitatingly say that we are successful because we are diverse. For instance, in the collections team, which is usually a male-dominated department, the stereotype is that one needs aggressive people. But given our customer-centricity and our focus to not hurt the brand with pushy collection practices, we knew that our collections team will need a different approach. Therefore, we went against the norm and hired more women in the team, many of whom are from a customer services background; they comprise 60 per cent of the team, and our head of quality control also happens to be a woman. This has led to better collection rates for us compared to our peers, resulting in a better bottom-line for the company. We hardly ever get any collection complaints. Our diversity has led to a very positive brand image for us. This makes recruitment quite easy, and also aids us in making business partnerships with banks on the one hand and with e-commerce companies on the other since they regard us as a partnership-friendly firm.

What is your view on gender inclusion when it comes to the tech and finance industry, which is male-dominated? And how do you implement it at ZestMoney?
When it comes to recruitment and hiring, my view is that gender should not even be a topic of consideration anymore; it should only be about one's capabilities. We

have achieved equal representation at ZestMoney with an almost 50:50 ratio at the organisational level. At the C-suite level, we are 60 per cent women. So, gender as an issue never comes up at ZestMoney. But we do realise the importance of women role models in maintaining this parity. Seeing women in senior and leadership roles helps other women to get there too. They get the confidence to chase their ambition with the thought, 'If she can do it, so can I.' We also acknowledge the fact that women take a disproportionate share of household responsibility, so we have adopted a flexible approach by allowing them to work from home over emails and video calls. Due to COVID-19, more companies are doing this now. I feel that this flexibility can help women stay in the workforce and aid the re-entry of women who have had to leave because of child-rearing responsibilities.

How do you achieve acceptance of diversity and inclusion across management levels?

As a leadership, we have zero tolerance for anyone who shifts our culture towards prejudice. We will fire anyone who makes any comment which is against our equality principles. In the past, when one of our employees passed a comment on skin colour, we made a big case study about it to ensure that all our employees know how sternly we look down on bias of any kind. I believe that acceptance of diversity and inclusion across levels is to a great extent a derivative of the founders' ethical compass. If the leadership focuses principally on work and rewards performance, there will be no bias and equality will happen organically. Often women feel that they will not get promoted because they don't have strong professional networks, but we focus on output at all times and reward merit and talent.

We maintain transparency at every important junction; recruitment, evaluations and promotions are very detailed and very transparent. Everything is process-oriented to rule out bias and favouritism. For instance, to become a senior VP, there are 12 defined specifications, and we evaluate all candidates up for promotion based on these criteria with objectivity. We are very data-driven with no room for subjectivity. We don't bend the rules on our established benchmarks to assess people. We maintain consistency. Due to the unprecedented business scenario created by COVID-19, we had to cut compensations and we did so with objectivity, without any opaqueness. We clearly defined and announced the percentage cut for each band of employees. Because of this approach, people trust us and have faith in the organisational system.

What are the gender-inclusion initiatives and policies at ZestMoney that you take pride in?

We follow the policy of prevention before cure. How do we ensure that women stay in the organisation long term and do not drop off in the middle of their careers? For this, we strongly work towards creating female role models at every level in the organisation, which gives a vision to other women that they too can have a career for life at ZestMoney. In the company, we work towards normalising being a working woman and a working mother. This gives young women a sense of confidence that we can accommodate their needs and support them to manage both personal and professional lives. For instance, we bring our kids to work for a day every quarter. It is well known that on most days, I try to leave the office by 6 PM so I can have dinner with my son. Having such an open culture helps women to stick around.

Additionally, given our focus on data, we also track monthly ratios across management levels, gender and age. We also study attrition and the reason behind it. If strong themes come to the fore in our analysis, we take corrective action.

What are some specific policies your organisation implements towards building a strong channel of women leaders?
Having valuable role models helps a lot. At ZestMoney, the women's group organises monthly events. We do multiple panel discussions where various issues are talked about openly—for instance, problems and challenges faced by working mothers. Women are more open and forthcoming in such group settings, and it builds strong relationships among them. We also keep an eye on high-potential women employees and define for them a career path upfront, so they can stay on with the company for the long run. One advice that I give to all women is that no matter which stage of life you are in—newly married, planning kids or a mother—talk about your job, your career with your spouse and your in-laws, otherwise they will never know how passionate you are about your work and that it is an important part of your life. It is quite commonly expected of women to quit their job once they get pregnant. Therefore, be vocal about your passion and your inclination to continue with your career. Only when we plug the leakage of women at mid-management levels can we build a strong pipeline of women candidates for senior roles.

10

Call by the Leadership

Let me start this chapter by reflecting on the conversation I had with one of the most successful leaders of our country, a phenomenal woman holding the position of MD of HDFC Ltd, a leading provider of housing finance in India—Renu Sud Karnad. HDFC Ltd is the pioneer of housing finance in India and has financed more than 8 million homes. It has a market cap of over US$60 billion.

#RainmakerSpeak

Renu Sud Karnad, MD, HDFC Ltd

Renu joined HDFC Ltd in 1978 and was elevated to the post of MD in 2010. As part of the management team, Renu has played an important role in the transformation of HDFC into India's leading financial services conglomerate by facilitating the formation of several companies, including HDFC Bank (India's leading private sector bank with a market cap of US$100 billion), HDFC Asset Management Company Ltd, HDFC Life Insurance Company Ltd, HDFC ERGO General Insurance Company Ltd, among others. Most of these companies are among the leaders in their respective fields.

Over the years, Renu has received numerous awards and accolades to her credit. To name a few, she was awarded the Outstanding Woman Business Leader award at the CNBC-TV18 Indian Business Leader Awards 2012. She was part of the 25 most influential women professionals in India, *India Today* magazine's power list 2011, and has featured in the *ET Corporate Dossier* list of India Inc's 'Top 15 Powerful Women CEOs' in 2010 and *Fortune India* magazine's most powerful women for 2011–2020.

Renu has been instrumental in building HDFC's retail network and has been at the forefront of digital transformation in the company. Apart from being HDFC's brand custodian, Renu is the guiding force behind the formulation of the organisation's communication strategy and public image.[1]

The leader's core philosophy

I had a focused interaction with Renu to understand her views on gender equality and inclusion as a leader and how she implements it in her organisation. The starting point was the core philosophy with which she operates.

Renu highlighted that the leader should believe in the potential of women and the value they can add to the business. It is not just about equal opportunity for women but about economic growth too. It is an often-cited fact that increasing women's labour force

[1] https://www.hdfc.com/sites/default/files/2019-07/renu-sud-karnad_9.pdf

participation by 10 percentage points could add US$770 billion to India's GDP by 2025.[2]

What Renu mentioned is in line with multiple research reports analysing the positive impact of gender diversity and inclusion on business performance globally. For instance, a report by Gallup found that having a combination of employee engagement and gender diversity improved financial outcomes for business units by 46 per cent (revenue) and 58 per cent (net profit).[3]

Thus, Renu very practically approaches gender equality with a business lens and encourages the same attitude among the managers in her organisation. During our conversation, she elaborated on her leadership style and how she propagates a culture of inclusion and fairness.

The power of dialogue

'I don't just impose certain percentages on managers (that they need to have x per cent women in their teams) but I try to bring a change in their attitude. For instance, I noticed that there were certain branch managers who would not hire a single woman in their teams. I didn't have to, but I would sit with them to reason it out with them.

[2] 'Women in the Workforce: India'. Catalyst, 28 October 2020. Available at: https://www.catalyst.org/research/women-in-the-workforce-india

[3] 'Three Requirements of a Diverse and Inclusive Culture and Why They Matter for Your Organization' (https://www.gallup.com/workplace/242108/diversity-inclusion-perspective-paper.aspx); 2018 Gallup Inc. All rights reserved.

'For example, a senior branch manager once told me that a woman is better suited for the role of a receptionist and not for core business operations. I knew this gentleman had a brilliant daughter who had just completed her engineering and was looking for a job. So, I asked him if his aspiration for his daughter was for her to be a receptionist? He very passionately said, "Of course not! She is brilliant and she will be joining as an engineer in one of the big IT firms." I reminded him that the girls who apply to our company also have such aspirations and they need to be given a chance and shown faith in. From that day on, there was a marked change in his behaviour. It has been many years, but even today, he remembers this conversation.

'It is up to the leader to sense the pulse of the organisation and to address gender inclusion not just through policies. Given employees may have their own deep-rooted biases, it is important to rationalise the same with open conversations—imposing policies will not be effective unless supplemented with education, open dialogue and cultivating the right culture throughout the organisation.'

Leading by example

'It is important for leaders to show, in their behaviour, the values they stand for. I have always maintained an assertive demeanour and I encourage all employees to be respectful and vocal. I am aware that women may face biases (often unconscious in nature) from their managers, peers and juniors. There may be instances where women's expertise at their job is unnecessarily questioned or their voice in a meeting is drowned out. In such situations, my mandate is clear—merit stands above all. Become the best at your job, know things inside out and then if anyone questions your authority or domain skills, be vocal and set the record straight. If you have mastered your work, don't take to any bias. I have observed that once a woman asserts command and superiority at work, people don't mess with her or look down upon her.'

Propagating a culture of openness

'Policies play a very important role to enable employees to continue with their career uninterrupted—be it the parental leave policy, flexible working options, mobility options, etc. But as a leader, what I also propagate in the organisation is a culture of openness, and we understand the needs of every employee we bring into our system. I want people to look at HDFC as a place where they can make a career for a lifetime if they choose to do so and for that, it is very important that the organisation understands their personal needs too.

'Hiring and performance evaluations are key areas where women are always second-guessing themselves. These are important times for most employees and what we try to do is to constantly reinforce our cultural beliefs at each stage.

'Starting with the hiring stage, I encourage all managers to lay it out for the candidates that the organisation will be supportive of their personal milestones and offer assistance for commitments like child care, ageing parents and crucial years of a child's education. The employee shouldn't be left questioning the company's commitment to employee well-being and should know that their organisation will respect their professional as well as personal needs. This is especially true for women since they continue to shoulder a disproportionate amount of caregiving responsibilities. If women know that their employer understands this and will ensure their personal commitments don't impact their career (and hiring, appraisals, promotions will all be solely dependent on their performance as a professional), then they will be able to give 100 per cent to their work. They will not be left thinking about leaving when they become mothers if they have the confidence that they will be able to integrate back into work after their maternity leave and the working environment will be welcoming for them.'

Endorsing mentorship

'As a leader, I endorse mentorship throughout the organisation. That is another tenet I strongly stand by. All the people who reach senior positions should share their experiences with the younger crop of professionals and help them in their journey. They should invest time and effort in training young professionals on the job and guide them through their careers.

'Most senior professionals believe in the same and do take efforts in this direction as they set the organisation for long-term success. But it is also important to note that unconscious bias may percolate their mentorship efforts as well. It is important to identify such biases and train people to be gender-sensitive (whether by way of policies, organisational awareness initiatives or as part of their own mentorship). Most of them have a wife and appreciate the efforts she puts in to run her professional and personal life in tandem, but organisational initiatives are very important to address conscious/unconscious biases which may emerge at the workplace. Incorporating gender inclusion in the outlook of managers towards mentorship will ensure that the organisation is able to build an empathetic culture towards the needs of women colleagues.'

Closing note: You can have it all, make sure you have the right environment

'As a closing thought, I would say that women today need to realise that it is possible to have it all. On the personal front, a supportive spouse and a family who believe in your potential as an individual are super important. On the professional front, being in an organisation whose leadership endorses gender equality and inclusion goes a long way.'

Allies in inclusive leaders

Don't just stand for the success of other women—insist on it.

—Gail Blanke

President and CEO, Gail Blanke's Lifedesigns

Following are some of India's most competent and successful women in the world of business and finance:

- Kalpana Morparia, former chairperson, South and South-East Asia, J.P. Morgan
- Renuka Ramnath, founder and CEO, Multiples Asset Management
- Zarin Daruwala, CEO, Standard Chartered Bank, India
- Madhabi Puri Buch, whole time member (WTM) of the Securities and Exchange Board of India (SEBI)
- Shikha Sharma, advisor to Google Pay India, former CEO, Axis bank
- Shilpa Kumar, partner at Omidyar Network India
- Lalita Gupte, independent director of ICICI Lombard General Insurance Company
- Vishakha Mulye, MD and CEO, ICICI Venture
- Anita Pai, COO, Yes Bank

They all have one thing in common—ICICI Bank. In the 1970s and 1980s, a time when gender inclusion was not a sought-after concept in the corporate world, ICICI was establishing itself as the most gender-neutral organisation in the world of banking and finance. Over the years, ICICI Bank not only became India's largest private sector bank, but it also established a name for itself in recognising and empowering female talent. The first woman who rose to a senior position at the bank was Lalita Gupte, who joined the organisation in 1971. The list of women leaders got longer and more formidable from then on, to a point where ICICI Bank emerged as a 'CEO factory' of primarily women leaders.[4] Today, all these talented women are spread across the industry, heading offices of giant MNCs or running their own funds and managing assets worth millions of dollars.

In recognising and mentoring their talents, the leadership at ICICI Bank played a major role. The organisational culture was shaped by the management in a way that it was truly gender-neutral in its outlook and actions. K.V. Kamath, CEO of ICICI Bank (1996–2009), on being asked about consistently choosing women over men for realising his vision for ICICI, mentioned that he never gave preference to women. It was only a result of merit and of not distinguishing between a man or a woman. His focus has always been to pick 'leaders with ability, intellect, and the entrepreneurial ability to lead teams', and he values women's 'ability to think in a much more detached manner than men'.[5] Kamath created a rare organisational culture, free of any gender bias, where women felt comfortable. He also approached mentoring quite consciously and worked towards helping young talent develop into well-rounded professionals. Kamath says:

> We had a large pool of people, most of them in their 30s, but none of them at seniority levels required by the organisation. I had to watch for talent and once I

[4] https://economictimes.indiatimes.com/how-icici-bank-has-emerged-as-a-ceo-factory-of-primarily-women-leaders/articleshow/31682254.cms?from=mdr

[5] https://archive.fortune.com/magazines/fortune/fortune_archive/2006/10/16/8390326/index.htm

> spotted it, it was my job to provide them opportunities to grow. Once they had reached a senior level, I then needed to rotate them through different areas so their talents were rounded. At the same time, mentoring is not a group exercise. Each one's need is different.[6]

This goes to show how important leadership endorsement is for a bias-free and inclusive culture. It's only when the leaders themselves start assigning priority to diversity and inclusion that some actual action is taken and the gap between policies and real implementation is bridged. When the top management shows commitment to mentoring women to climb the echelons of success, the responsibility cascades down to all managers within the organisation. This thought clearly emerged as a common theme in all my interactions with several exemplary women.

To help achieve a gender-neutral culture, I have identified a three-pronged approach that can support the leadership in turning their gender-inclusive vision into reality at their respective organisations.

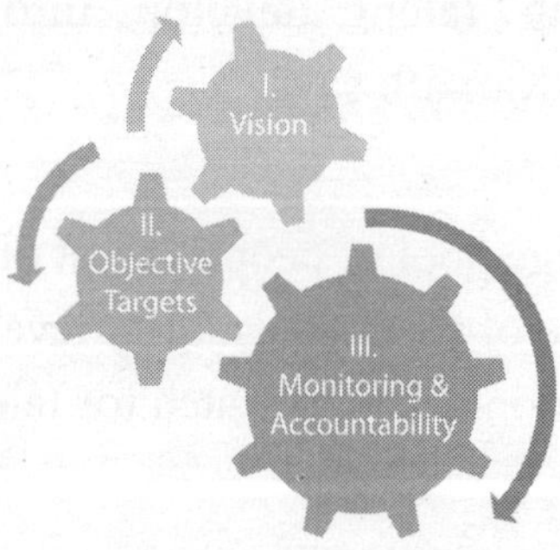

[6] https://economictimes.indiatimes.com/what-makes-kv-kamath-india-incs-most-prolific-ceo-guru/articleshow/12637350.cms

Vision

The first step for a leader is to ascertain their honest stand on gender inclusion and assess how committed they are to drive it in their organisation. To determine this, they need to ask themselves the following question and answer it earnestly: Do I, as the leader/CEO of my organisation, endorse the viewpoint of equal participation by women at each level in my company? Do I see a real value addition in terms of culture and financial performance by having women occupy senior and important roles?

Unless the answer to this two-part question is 'Yes', the organisation will struggle to achieve real inclusiveness across levels. Diversity and inclusion cannot be dealt with by the HR department alone; it has to be accepted as a combined responsibility by the head of each department. Unless the leadership openly endorses gender inclusion and commits to achieving it as seriously as they commit to financial targets, there will remain a gap in inclusion policies and their implementation. Thus, the CEO, in her or his vision for the company, should include the view on diversity and must communicate the same to the organisation as a whole. This will bring in a sense of commitment towards achieving the publicly proclaimed word.

This became quite clear during my interaction with Devjani Goswami Sharma, talent and organisational development head, Sodexo India. She acknowledged the vital role played by the leadership's vision in driving gender-inclusion initiatives. She mentioned that at

Sodexo, the agenda of equality is driven top-down. Based on their leadership's commitment, they have developed the Better Tomorrow 2025 commitments, and one of the focus areas of this initiative is gender equality. They have an advisory board, SoTogether, working on achieving gender balance at all levels. Given the top brass's effort towards achieving gender equality, everyone in the organisation is vested in achieving it.

Objective targets

For a vision to translate into reality, implementable steps need to be defined for its achievement. In addition to the enabling policies, which we will discuss in detail in later chapters, it is important that the CEO's vision on gender inclusion is translated into objective, measurable targets, which are then allocated to the respective HoDs and the HR team. For example, Sodexo's SoTogether advisory board, which works on achieving gender balance at all levels, has defined specific objectives such as 40 per cent women leaders by 2025, improvement in gender balance across management teams, among others.

Once the objectives are defined, it is important for the organisation to work towards achieving them; they need to be further broken into implementable steps across all levels. All relevant stakeholders in the company have to contribute towards this aim. At Sodexo, for people in managerial positions and in senior roles, KPIs include gender and inclusion targets, in hiring (overall composition, internal hiring and promotions), as well as training and development. This ensures clear, defined targets at each level for the successful implementation of organisational objectives.

Monitoring and accountability

The leadership should monitor the pulse of the organisation and take steps if things are not going in the right direction. There are small cues one can easily pick up on. For instance, Marc Benioff, chair, CEO and founder of Salesforce, mentioned in one of his interviews that when he noticed that most executive management meetings had only male attendees, he made a rule that a minimum of one-third of participants at such meetings should be women. Many companies have now started to observe how many women participants are there in important meetings, how they are conducting themselves, if they are only taking notes or actively participating, how the men in the room are responding to their inputs, etc. Such measures will surely contribute towards creating more balanced work cultures.

Then comes the role of accountability in ensuring a bias-free organisation. Unless the suggested targets are measured and the HoDs and people in HR are held accountable for these targets, the needle will sadly continue to move at a slow pace. Also, there's limited point in analysing things post facto unless done with the right spirit. Many organisations end up discussing a shortfall in women participation during year-end meetings but do nothing to lay down concrete steps in order to improve on this parameter in the years to come. Such half-hearted measures result in wasted efforts and no more.

Taking a cue from Will Craig's thought, 'Accountability is the glue that bonds commitment to results'[7], it is important that the CEO attaches accountability to diversity-and-inclusion targets. The progress on these targets needs to be monitored, just like the progress on financial targets is tracked. Maybe every quarter, the HoDs and the HR can present objective, quantifiable numbers on how they have progressed on recruiting women across levels, female attrition across levels and the number of women in the pipeline for key roles. All of these need to be laid out and discussed along with the financial performance of the company. Each business head should be accountable for their respective department's progress on diversity and inclusion, supported by the HR team.

It is only when people see that the CEO of the company is taking a keen interest in turning the vision of an inclusive company into a reality that everybody will be moved to take action to achieve the desired targets on creating a bias-free and all-embracing work environment.

Another possible and effective way to implement this could be to attach monetary measures to this agenda. A percentage of a discretionary bonus pool or variable pay of each line of business could be linked to the performance of that business on the diversity

[7] Craig, W. 2017. *Living the Hero's Journey*. Live and Learn Publishing.

and inclusion targets. The carrot should work in this case. Sodexo has already put this into practice; it has linked management incentives, including 10 per cent of bonuses, to achieving gender goals.[8] As soon as numbers come into play, accountability is set in motion more firmly.

To sum up, the onus of setting the right tone on diversity-and-inclusion agenda lies with the leadership team. As they start holding themselves accountable for the same set of inclusion targets, the same behaviour will flow down throughout the organisation. Thus, the leadership brass can proudly walk the talk on diversity and inclusion and see their vision getting translated into reality.

#InclusionStalwart

Sodexo

With powerful internal gender balance measures and a strong focus on inclusion, Sodexo's commitment to gender equality is at the heart of its strategy and performance. Learning more about the company helped me gain insights into an organisation's gender-inclusion policies and the role leadership can play in influencing and shaping these policies.

Founded in 1966, Sodexo is a world leader in providing food services and facilities management: from reception, maintenance and cleaning facilities to in-home assistance, childcare centres and concierge services. With worldwide consolidated revenue of

[8] 'Sodexo's Gender Balance Study 2018'; Copyright (c) 2018 Sodexo Operations, LLC. Sourced with permission.

€22 billion in 2019, Sodexo serves 100 million consumers daily, across 67 countries around the globe. Sodexo is among the top 20 private employers worldwide, employing close to half a million people. It is an organisation where the implementation of gender-neutral policies is not just limited to paper but is visibly practised through the company, with women comprising 35 per cent of Sodexo's executive committee and 60 per cent of its board of directors. By 2025, Sodexo's goal is to have at least 40 per cent women representatives as part of its senior leadership staff.

I had the opportunity of conversing with Devjani Goswami Sharma, talent and organisational development head, Sodexo, India. Devjani is a seasoned HR professional, with a rich and diverse experience of handling large and geographically broad teams across several organisations.

What are some key messages from your leadership on their vision for gender inclusion, and what are you doing to make this vision a reality?

Leadership plays a vital role in driving gender-inclusion initiatives in any organisation. At Sodexo, the gender-equality agenda is driven top-down. In 2017, Sodexo OSS (On Site Services) signed the Women's Empowerment Principles (WEPs) charter, committing to drive seven key principles:

- Establish high-level corporate leadership for gender equality
- Treat all women and men fairly at work—respect and support human rights and non-discrimination

- Ensure the health, safety and well-being of all women and men workers
- Promote education, training and professional development for women
- Implement enterprise-development, supply chain and marketing practices that empower women
- Promote equality through community initiatives and advocacy
- Measure and publicly report on progress to achieve gender equality

Our leadership's commitment to the equality agenda is well recognised both internally and externally. Internally, we have developed Better Tomorrow 2025 commitments, and one of the focus areas of Better Tomorrow is gender equality. We have a SoTogether advisory board working on achieving gender balance at all levels. Its objectives include:

- Around 40 per cent women leaders by 2025
- Increase women in the talent pipeline
- Increase gender balance in management teams
- Increase the number of women in operations
- Create a culture of inclusion

Our management's inclination to building a workplace that is suitable for women is also visible with them being a part of Catalyst, a global non-profit organisation working towards accelerating progress for women at work. Our CEO, Denis Machuel, is on the board of directors of Catalyst.

Everyone in the organisation is vested in the belief of achieving equality. The equality metric is tracked in all the performance reviews, thus adding accountability to the targets.

Have you seen the actual benefits of gender inclusion at Sodexo?
Absolutely. We, at Sodexo, believe that when women are empowered, we are all empowered. Gender equality enhances our performance and creates a better tomorrow for all our stakeholders—employees, clients, consumers and the communities that we serve. Our internal research shows that gender-balanced teams perform better on multiple fronts. They report better numbers in several areas: operating margins, employee retention, client retention, employee engagement and safety. All of this contributes to the better performance of organisation and builds up a strong brand.

Sodexo has been included in the Bloomberg's GEI in both 2019 and 2020, which recognises our commitment to supporting gender equality through policy development, representation and transparency.

What are some of the best practices encouraged at Sodexo towards inculcating a respectful and merit led culture, free of gender stereotypes?
Our leadership's commitment to gender equality flows down to all the employees across levels. For people in managerial positions and in senior roles, KPIs include gender and inclusion targets, with regard to hiring (overall composition, internal hiring and promotions), as well as development. It is a must to have one woman in our final shortlist for all positions rolled out internally or externally. We also have incentive schemes for managers, which are paid out if they have the right

diversity ratio and have hired women employees. We ensure that appraisals and promotions are done fairly and are driven by meritocracy. Our well-defined KPI system ensures the same. We diligently track women who are in our HiPo (High Potential) list across levels and have regular career aspiration discussions with them to prevent any avoidable attrition.

For peers and juniors, a respectful culture towards all is promoted. We pay attention to semantics as well. For instance, as an organisation, we do not have any designations that are gender-specific. In our industry, we have designations like 'house maid', 'bell boy', etc., but we have scrapped all such designations and they are all now gender-neutral. In our day-to-day informal discussions too, we refrain from using words such as 'guys'. There is complete flexibility when it comes to working, whether it is permanent, temporary or part-time employment. In addition, we have work-from-home options as well. We encourage employees to not judge each other based on the type of work arrangement they may have. As long as quality work is being delivered, we are good to go!

Which are the gender inclusion initiatives at Sodexo that you would take pride in?

The list runs long here, but let me name a few. The Better Tomorrow 2025 commitments is a great initiative, focused on having more women in leadership roles and in general increasing the female talent pipeline. We also have mentoring networks for women, as part of which one gets access to women mentors spread across different geographies that we operate in. We call it the SoTogether Mentoring Program.

We are very diligent in tracking our women exits, especially those of HiPo women, across levels. All exits of women employees are tracked and reviewed on a monthly basis. The diversity-and-inclusion head has a conversation with all HiPo and promotable women who resign.

Women safety is given a lot of importance. We have an SOS button available on our portal. If one clicks on that, a message goes to the reporting manager and the HR business partner. Within 10 minutes, the person gets a call from them to enquire about their safety.

Even for our engagement studies, we cull out a slice on what our female employees have to say on every engagement parameter and analyse that separately for specific action plans.

We have good referral schemes encouraging women referrals across levels. We have a programme called 'Win-Back', through which we tap our ex-employees and stay in touch with them, and whenever they are ready, we hire them back. We also encourage spouses to be hired, as it brings in more loyalty towards the organisation and more support for the employee.

11

The Role of Reporting Managers

'Forty-nine per cent managers say choosing a male over an equally meritorious female candidate is better strategy ... Fifty-four per cent say women should take a career break when work-life integration turns demanding ... Forty-nine per cent say managing teams with women is challenging.'[1]

Bias and scepticism among managers is a key barrier to the success of any gender-inclusion initiative. It is especially important, considering a manager's role in shaping careers. They hire employees, are responsible for their ongoing work profile, coach them through career development and manage appraisals. While the top leadership may have a vision and the HR department policies in place, there are always unsaid micro-policies that an immediate boss encourages. These may differ from one manager to the next, but they impact hiring and promotions. Given the importance of their roles, people often follow the adage 'Choose a boss, not a job'. A great boss can help you unlock untapped potential, while an average boss can demoralise you.

[1] https://economictimes.indiatimes.com/news/company/corporate-trends/how-regressive-attitudes-towards-gender-inclusion-are-deeply-entrenched-in-corporate-spaces/articleshow/74531111.cms

Learning and development

Payal Gupta, director and CEO of the consulting firm Celebratory Network, shared an instance during our discussion which aptly demonstrates how sensitisation through learning and development (L&D) programmes is crucial for managers:

> We consulted with a company where a chairperson, who had called a meeting of all the senior MDs, asked the only woman present in the group to take notes, not acknowledging the fact that she was the business lead of the largest line of business. He just assumed that the woman would take notes. Sensitisation through L&D programmes to stop such behaviour is essential and all managers should go through it.

While most HR teams focus on sensitisation of managers through training and development initiatives, it is equally important to ensure real implementation of some of the learnings. One aspect which is criticised by some business heads is that most training sessions tend to be clichéd, irrelevant to their job, with little focus on business. For a more suitable engagement, the HR team must engage with department heads and work together to create business-specific training programmes.

Beyond training in soft skills like empathy and understanding comes the aspect of mentoring and creating leaders, which needs the time and attention of managers. While most managers do take some time out to mentor their juniors, it is limited to a performance discussion and a goal-setting exercise. Having a formal mentoring programme with direct bosses and other group heads can be impactful, if done right. Different organisations do it in different ways. An effective programme would be the practice of sponsorships, which are quite common in the consulting industry. Rightly implemented, sponsorships can prove to be a powerful tool. A mentor (usually not the reporting manager) represents their mentee on important platforms, gives them exposure to their own network, presents their case during appraisals and promotions, and gives real-time feedback on both performance and soft skills. This requires regular commitment on the part of the mentor to see their protégé rise through the levels, not just by giving advice, but by allocating one's own time and effort to the cause. Some companies promote this system by encouraging networking events that help their employees interact with members of different teams, clients and industry leaders and, in the process, find their respective mentors informally.

Another aspect of L&D is to coach employees in softer skills such as public speaking and critical thinking, and conduct mentoring sessions to provide appropriate career guidance and counselling. Had Kalpana Morparia's bosses not believed in her capabilities and pushed her to go beyond her comfort zone, she may not have been able to achieve the heights of success she has seen. Like Kalpana, many more women will be able to polish and enhance their skills and move ahead in the corporate world if they find supportive bosses.

Setting objective targets and processes

L&D is important, and several large organisations have 'Managerial Essentials Training' for awareness on gender inclusion. However, translating the concept of such awareness into real action is a daunting task. A structured approach, along with setting objective targets and processes across all aspects of a corporate journey, can help overcome the challenge. Broadly, there are three different stages across a corporate journey where women will benefit from having inclusive guidelines and goals in place: recruitment, daily work and performance appraisals.

First stumbling block: Recruitment

The discrimination that women face at the workplace usually begins at the interview itself, where the interviewer often comes in with preconceptions and set views. Women are then subjected to certain questions during an interview which men typically don't get asked, such as:

'What are your plans after marriage? How will you juggle your work and home?'

'How will you manage long working hours with motherhood? Do you see your drive and commitment being compromised?'

'She's qualified and has the required experience, but she's 30 and has no children yet…'

'She is a young mother and this role requires late nights and travelling, I don't think she will be able to do it.'

Such beliefs held by interviewers are, regrettably, not that uncommon. While hiring for entry-level jobs, these biased opinions are not as rampant. Hence, we continue to see 40 to 50 per cent women being hired at the entry level, especially in the services sector. But as we move up the ladder, the bias in hiring women starts coming to the fore. Many interviewers have mental blocks about hiring women of child-bearing age, while men do not get subjected to such issues related to personal milestones.

During my conversation with Payal, we spoke about what organisations can do to ensure bias-free hiring. She recalled a project they did with a manufacturing unit. The attendees were divided into two groups to interview potential employees. The first group was supposed to interview only men, and the second group had a mix of male and female candidates. Payal noticed that the questions the second group had lined up for the interviewees had much to do with their personal lives, such as plans after marriage and parenthood. The first focus group said such questions were not relevant. Payal recognised the unconscious bias that was at play, as a result of which women were being evaluated not just on their capability to do the job, but they were also being judged on their gender. Based on her interactions with the employees, Payal advised the organisation to follow a standard set of question-buckets, a process called 'behavioural event interviews' for all the candidates, to ensure that the evaluation remained fair, based on merit and not dependent on the interviewer's preconceived notions of a gendered ideal employee.

In order to remove prejudices at the interview stage, putting certain guardrails on the hiring process can help. Beyond awareness and education, creating a structured process for the interviewers is also important. Some organisations set specific objectives and guidelines against which all candidates are assessed and help track interviewer responses on those specific aspects. These objectives can also be a negative list of what not to focus on during hiring. This helps to ensure a focused hiring approach and reduce biases to a large extent. When interviewers have a specific task at hand, they tend to remain disciplined in their approach to hiring.

Finally, it helps to get views of people with different backgrounds and working styles for a bias-free hiring process. Therefore, it should be ensured that the interview panel consists of a diverse set of individuals, including women. A fair and unbiased hiring process is the first step towards ensuring an equal opportunities workplace.

Dealing with the routine: Daily work

Getting a chance to execute good, high-level work contributes to the development of an employee, and a capable manager needs to enable this for all team members. Thus, as a self-check, all managers should see that the important, analytical projects are distributed equitably in the team, to avoid instances where strategic projects end up falling in a man's lap while the woman on the team ends up managing more mundane and operational projects.

Let's understand this with Anita's case study.

Anita is among the few women who have made it in the field of corporate investing. When she joined Organisation A, she was reporting directly to the head of business (HOB), Samar Mittal. As months passed, she developed a very good rapport with him and proved her mettle through her hard work and key insights on projects. Her conduct and maturity at work were clearly beyond her years of experience and Samar acknowledged this fact.

After a year, the organisation underwent some restructuring and a new HOB, Dev Rao, was brought on board. Anita had a good working relation with him as well. But, within a few months of working with him, she could gauge how different his thinking was. Dev was 56 years old; he had spent all his life working in India, with no global exposure. There was no doubt he was good at what he did, with many industrial accolades to his credit, but he had always worked in male-dominated fields, finance being one such. Even at Organisation A, there were very few women in front-end revenue-generating roles.

This was in contrast with the earlier HOB, Samar Mittal's profile. Samar was the same age as Dev, but he had a very diverse work experience; he had spent close to three decades working in MNCs across the globe. This exposure to different cultures and working styles was clearly evident in Samar's management approach. He was very thoughtful and judged his team and people only by their calibre. For him, gender was not a factor at all and this showed in his day-to-day dealings with everyone.

Though Dev tried to adopt a more open and inclusive style of working, he was unable to act outside his social conditioning where he was more comfortable with and more trusting of the work done by male team members. In some of the team meetings he would invite Anita, but in most of the strategic meetings, her name would not even occur to Dev. This was hampering Anita's growth and learning as a professional since she was being excluded from the big-picture discussions.

Many women in corporate India face similar situations—being denied equal opportunities, compared to their male counterparts, puts their chances of reaching the leadership level in jeopardy. In such cases, the performance of the male colleague could be better simply because of the advantage of getting better responsibilities and exposure. As an impartial employer, ICICI Bank ensures that men and women get equal chances, and late sittings do not interfere in the participation levels of women.

'[While] preparing a list of employees attending a brainstorming session, that may go into the wee hours of the morning, a management trainee might consider the timings odd and deliberately not include the names of his female batchmates. He is then, corrected by his seniors and made aware that the organisation expects the entire team to be present. This makes him realise, that women do not need to be treated any differently,'[2] says Amitabh Chaturvedi, ex-GM, Retail Liabilities, ICICI Bank.

The requirement, therefore, is to have a sensitised and neutral top brass who can get the most out of young talent and nurture them, giving them opportunities to grow and explore. Beyond that, organisations should look at

[2] https://www.financialexpress.com/archive/first-among-equals-icicis-woman-power/74949/

ways to ensure that equal exposure and responsibilities are available for all the employees. There cannot be a standardised approach to this. Some investment banks manage this by having a common pool of analysts and associates and a separate staffer responsible for the allocation of resources and teams. Some other companies follow rotation policies for different projects and teams, especially for their leadership programmes, which help all employees gain similar training, at least in the initial stages as they find their feet in the organisation.

Performance evaluations

Men tend to be evaluated on potential, while managers demand proven accomplishments from women. Men are also likely to get more credit for their success compared to women. To add to this joy-ride, women are judged more critically for any failures. This creates an uneven playing field for them.

Women continue to struggle more for promotions at managerial levels and beyond. For every 100 men promoted as managers, only 85 women get promoted. Largely because of this disparity, men end up with 62 per cent of manager-level positions, while women hold only 38 per cent of such roles.[3]

[3] 'Women in the Workplace 2020', September 2020, McKinsey & Company, www.mckinsey.com; Copyright (c) 2021 McKinsey & Company. All rights reserved. Reprinted by permission. 'Women in the Workplace' is the largest comprehensive study of the state of women in corporate America. Since 2015, McKinsey & Company and *LeanIn.Org* have published this report annually to give companies and employees the information they need to advance women and improve gender diversity within their organisations.

The ratio only gets worse thereafter. Continued biases at work end up slowing the career graph of women by several crucial years. If we want to close the current, significant gender gap, women need to be evaluated fairly and on an equal footing as men.

An objective evaluation system plays the most important role in removing biases during performance appraisals. This was made clear by several industry leaders and HR professionals I met. Setting clear targets is the answer. When employees know the KPIs they are working towards and the level of performance that will take them forward, subjective opinions can be kept at bay. ZestMoney is one company where this system is followed and transparency and consistency are maintained during all evaluations.

Payal Gupta stressed the importance of having an audit of the performance evaluation process by citing advice she gave one of her clients. She said, 'Managers need to be given formal training in carrying out fair evaluations and giving feedback. Post these trainings, there needs to be a panel that checks how managers are doing reviews—this panel can sit in random selections of appraisals to gauge the effectiveness of manager evaluation training. Additionally, feedback needs to be gathered from subordinates on the quality of the review discussion. They should get a sense that their manager invested time in preparing their feedback, highlighted their strengths and gave specific inputs for areas of improvement. Where the quality of review feedback is consistently poor for any manager, the panel should take corrective steps through rigorous training in helping the manager improve.'

A good boss paves the way for future good bosses

For an inclusive work environment, an organisation needs to train and sensitise its managers in the right way and promote a culture of objectivity across the board. It is the HR team's responsibility to track diversity-and-inclusion targets for each manager and undertake proactive interventions when they see a dip in performance on these parameters. The company's assertiveness in holding managers accountable for gender inclusion is a key pillar of how effectively policy is translated into meaningful actions and results.

12

Cheer from Peers

Any society that fails to harness the energy and creativity of its women is at a huge disadvantage in the modern world.

—Tian Wei

Former Washington correspondent and currently the host of *World Insight with Tian Wei* on CGTN

Despite requisite sensitisation trainings at an organisational level, the divide within heterogeneous teams often comes to the fore. Women continue to struggle against gender disparity and are unable to contribute to their full potential. Nearly 34 per cent of women who work in male-dominated environments acknowledge that their gender has had a negative impact on their work.[1] A McKinsey report shows the kind of biases women continue to face at the workplace. If women keep getting questioned about their competence and commitment, it leads to a waste of time and talent, costing the organisation in the long run.

[1] https://www.pewresearch.org/fact-tank/2018/03/07/women-in-majority-male-workplaces-report-higher-rates-of-gender-discrimination/

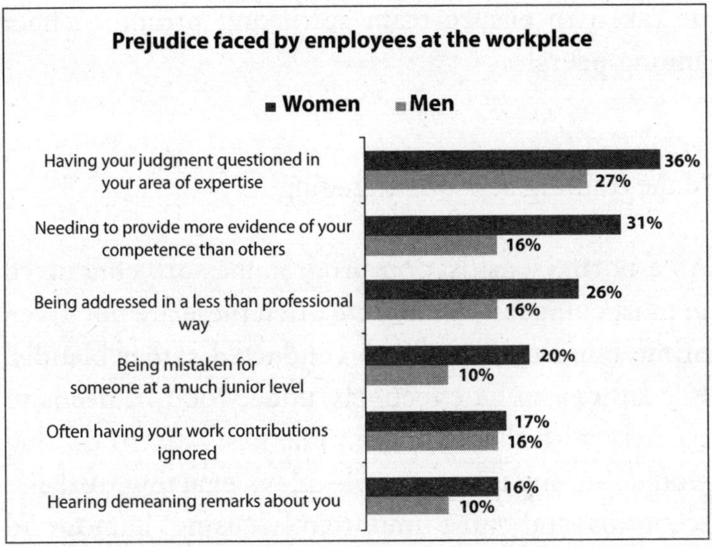

[2]

'An insurance company which wanted to improve its organisational gender inclusion asked us to help them in creating a women's committee where female employees could network, seek career guidance and discuss any specific issues concerning them. Very soon, the men in the organisation began to feel uncomfortable about this committee and made jokes about it. This resulted in many women not joining the community because of the distasteful fun being made by their male peers,' recalled development consultant and coach, Payal Gupta.

A sense of camaraderie and respect among peers is imperative for a healthy work culture to prevail in any organisation. For improved productivity of employees that translates to better business performance, let's focus on some measures that can

[2] 'Women in the Workplace 2018', McKinsey & Company, www.mckinsey.com;

be taken to ensure team spirit and promote cheer among peers!

Make training sessions engaging

As a norm, sensitisation programmes are conducted in most companies, but quite often these are not given prime importance and are conducted rather blandly. For an idea to be effectively understood, it needs to connect with the audience. The best way to do that would be engaging in role play, enacting real-life scenarios and most importantly, using humour to pique the interest level of employees and get a serious message across. Often people absorb an idea better when it is delivered through a participative medium. While talking about gender inclusion training done at J.P. Morgan, Kalpana Morparia mentioned how role-playing activities conducted during Universal Women's Week were most impactful in making people aware of subconscious bias and helped in changing conservative mindsets.

Say goodbye to favouritism

Team dynamics and camaraderie are often a replication of the organisation's culture. Positive energies in a team help with smoother working relations and better productivity. Prerna Parija, head, enterprise business, at Zomato, maintains that impartial assessment and recognition by the boss lead to friendly and cordial peer relations. 'In some teams, I have seen great camaraderie while in some, there is groupism. In all my teams, I have mostly seen great bonding and an open culture amongst the team members, both male and female. Personally, I haven't done anything differently for female members in my team, I have just treated them as equals (just as I would expect from my manager). When women see themselves as true equals, they feel empowered. I believe in being empathetic yet fair to everyone, irrespective of their gender. This fosters the right culture for growth for every team member and for the organisation at large. Also, when there's fairness in the system with no favouritism towards either gender, it leads to a healthy work environment within the peer group,' elaborated Prerna.

Biology, equality, normalcy

In the corporate world, women are always outnumbered by men. This creates a more masculine culture, where men stay in their cohorts while women self-consciously tiptoe around their own biology. This widens the male–female divide at a peer level. To address this issue, both men and women need to take some steps. First, women need to feel comfortable in their own skin and not be apologetic for their gender. What we go through biologically, whether it is menstruation or pregnancy, are natural processes, as normal as breathing. If during this time, any woman needs additional help, she should be able to receive it without feeling self-conscious.

Doing away with this hesitation will go a long way in preventing avoidable attrition of women when they are feeling overwhelmed with personal and professional commitments.

A corporate career is long-running like a marathon, spanning nearly 40 years. In that context, if an employee needs the organisation's support of a few months or a couple of years for personal milestones, they should receive it without being judged. Equality goes both ways, and when women see men availing the benefits of supportive organisational policies, they too will feel more comfortable asking for assistance. ICICI Bank remains foremost as a supportive organisation, accommodative of a deserving employee's needs, be it a study break or a leave to look after sick parents.[3] Another example is of Zomato, which recently announced its menstrual leave policy, leading to many discussions on professional forums. As Prerna elaborated:

'There are biological differences between men and women—only a woman can bear a child, only a woman can have periods—and hence, the differences have to be respected for organisations to leverage women's capabilities to the maximum. The policy announcement on menstrual leave has been one of the most liberating moments as a working woman. The period leave destigmatises the perfectly normal phenomenon of menstruation. I, or any other woman in Zomato, no longer has to hesitantly give the reason

[3] https://www.financialexpress.com/archive/first-among-equals-icicis-woman-power/74949/

of poor health for managing this monthly occurrence. We can finally be open about it and plan our work better. I intend to avail it myself in the needful hour and be totally normal with my peers or juniors when they apply for one. Such openness creates a culture of understanding among peers. Not only this, Zomato had previously introduced six months' paternity leave realising that men and women share equal responsibilities while bringing up a newborn child.'

Therefore, when organisations treat both genders equally and give them need-based support and assistance, it creates a friendly culture where there is no resentment stemming from any preferential treatment meted out to one set over the other. This harnesses equality and recognises people as individuals who have personal lives that need organisational support from time to time.

The power of networking

To enhance peer relations, the other important aspect to address is networking. Normally, men involve themselves in daily networking activities like team drinks, cigarette breaks and tea breaks. Women are mostly missing from these scenes. Eventually, reporting managers and seniors join these quick breaks where male banter dominates and helps develop camaraderie. During such breaks, people not only discuss their personal lives, hobbies, their partners, children, etc., but they also end up discussing work, certain aspects that are not discussed in formal meetings. If women only remain part of the official meetings, they miss out on the chance to develop team rapport built through networking. The whole execution of the principle of inclusion takes a beating here, and all that stays is the hard glass ceiling that women continue to fight against. Payal Gupta mentioned that at several client organisations they implement the concept of 'Time, Task and Territory', where employees are encouraged to discuss only work-related matters during working hours, within the office premises, so that each stakeholder can be a part of all discussions. Payal also suggested creating conversation circles for leaders and senior management where they address both male and female employees and talk about their life stories, important learnings, challenges, vulnerabilities, etc. Through these conversation circles, women get exposure to the leadership, and they start developing a rapport with their peers and seniors attending these events.

Another suggestion to improve team dynamics is for members to step out together once a day for lunch or a coffee break. This can act as their daily dose of informal catch-up, where they can engage in informal discussions. In addition to the team events organised by the department, colleagues can make most of these daily opportunities and interact with their peers.

You say only what you know, but when you listen, you get to know so much you may have been unaware of. This value addition augments the charm of peer interactions; hence, indulge in team building in its true sense and have open free-flowing conversations outside of work.

Smartness in togetherness

We have had enough literature that shows how women have a different approach towards problem-solving than men. When team members have more inclusive discussions, their cognitive skills also improve. Additionally, decisions taken after such brainstorming sessions are more comprehensive, thanks to the inputs coming from different individuals with different perspectives. For instance, in strategy discussions, I have noticed that men often think in terms of the top and bottom line in the near to medium term. But they miss out on the underlying nuances to achieve these numbers—important factors are often sidelined like human capital, attrition and new hires, optimum organisation structure, investment into critical support functions like HR, operations, IT, risk management, etc. Women on the table can steer the discussion into covering these important topics.

Thus, to maximise an organisation's performance and have a smarter crop of employees, gender inclusion is the way forward. All that is needed is regular sensitisation training sessions, appropriate networking opportunities, informal team catch-ups and implementation of organisational policies that destigmatise gender-related differences.

#RainmakerSpeak

Sukhleen Aneja, chief marketing officer and marketing director, Reckitt Benckiser Hygiene, South Asia

Sales and marketing remains an interesting area for women. On one hand, 53 per cent entrepreneurs in the Indian direct selling industry are women,[4] but on the other hand, women continue to lag behind when it comes to holding the top job in marketing in the corporate world. Just like other C-suite roles, chief marketing officer (CMO) positions are also occupied mostly by men. For instance, the BW Top 50 Marketers 2021[5] list had only 10 women leaders. This 20 per cent representation shows that there is great scope for improvement. I got the opportunity to interact with one of the leaders featured in the list, Sukhleen Aneja, CMO and marketing director, Reckitt Benckiser Hygiene, South Asia.

Sukhleen has over 17 years of rich experience managing various businesses across FTSE Top 10 and Fortune 100 companies—Unilever, Reckitt Benckiser and L'Oréal. In her current role with Reckitt Benckiser, she focuses on marquee brands such as Harpic and Lysol. Most recently, Sukhleen has featured in the 'Asia-Pacific Power List 2021' as one of the region's 50 most influential marketers. In the past, she was recognised as one of *IMPACT's* 'Top 50 Most Influential Women

[4] https://www.business-standard.com/article/current-affairs/53-entrepreneurs-in-indian-direct-selling-industry-are-women-report-118081900435_1.html

[5] http://everythingexperiential.businessworld.in/article/The-Debut-Edition-of-BW-Top-50-Marketers-2021-Underlines-the-Rise-Of-Women-Marketing-Leaders/22-02-2021-380415/

in Business', 2019, listed in the *ET* 'Women Ahead' list amongst the 'Top 25 Rising Leaders in India 2019', and was also honoured in *ET*'s '40 under Forty' hottest professionals list for the year 2018.

During our interaction, Sukhleen drew on her personal experiences and how these shaped her as a professional who is passionate about augmenting inclusion. She had refreshing thoughts on the role organisations and leadership can play in helping women succeed in breaking the proverbial glass ceiling, especially in moving from mid-management to senior roles. Let us dive into the details.

Defining moments and key learnings

'I started my career in sales back in 2004 with Hindustan Unilever Limited, where as part of my first assignment I was given the opportunity to lead sales in the premium personal care division in Uttar Pradesh. The resident belief then was to give upcountry territory assignments to new joiners from metro cities so they could learn how to handle business and get accustomed to real India. There was utmost care taken for the employees' safety while giving them a launchpad to learn tremendously early on in their career. This role was a defining experience for me as I faced different challenges. I was in my early 20s, leading a predominantly male team in their mid-40s to early 50s. They were not accustomed to a woman in this role, and it took me some time to show them that I meant business.

'The market was extremely fragmented from a trade standpoint, and I travelled through almost 80 towns in a span of 3 months. During my travels, I noticed there were so many women who hadn't stepped beyond a 100-feet periphery of their houses—their world was limited to raising their family. This made me value my education and financial independence all the more. It also gave me a sense of gratefulness for the opportunities that I was given.

'The other stint that defined me professionally was my marketing assignment on Lakmé. Beauty at that time was just coming of age as a segment. I had the fortitude of launching Absolute, which was the premium end of Lakmé. This was way back in 2011. As part of developing Absolute, we spent a lot of time doing consumer research, and we came across the stereotypes associated with colour. For instance, a woman wearing red lipstick can be perceived in three different ways, from being provocative to being fashion-forward to perhaps someone who is trying too hard to grab attention. That a colour can make such a statement was a huge realisation!

'We also understood that women in India had been conditioned to believe in natural beauty. While they wanted to hide their flaws and look beautiful, they dared not stand out because there was fear and stigma associated with standing out, especially in the professional context, where women of course want to be recognised for fantastic work but not for being a woman. That is why a lot of times the symbols of professional success end up becoming more masculine, creating a corporate arena of blue, black and grey, or maternal, where women focus on highlighting traits that are more expected from them like compassion, patience, etc. Through these insights, I closely understood how we consciously or unconsciously brand people even without knowing them. That was the day when I said, "You know what, it's all upon us!" There is really no reason for us to feel any less in expressing our personality just because we are trying to fit in with the majority. We can be extremely successful by being our true self.

'I hope that more women become such role models who give the confidence to other women to bring their whole selves to work and who are not forced to hide a part of their personality. This also improves the organisational culture. Culture at the end of the day is what we choose to put up with and also what we personify and embody that makes it easier for others to thrive. So, bring your best personality and wholesome self to work.'

Placing choices in the hands of women

'I have always had a personal passion for improving women's representation within the teams I have worked in, and today I can proudly say that 55 to 60 per cent of my team comprises women who are spread across the levels, occupying junior to senior roles.

'I would like to highlight that this is not an overnight accomplishment; it took me a series of conscious decisions, especially to protect women from getting off the professional path in the middle of their careers when they take on the responsibilities of motherhood. Let me share an instance here when one of my team members was coming back from her maternity leave. We chose to put her on one of the most coveted assignments as against giving her a transition assignment, which a lot of times organisations give to a returning mother in an attempt to help her. But this option of seeking help should really be an employee's choice.

'I believe that by giving someone who is returning from a sabbatical a very coveted job, you set an example for others in the organisation too and give them the confidence that maternity will not adversely impact their career. Back then, allocating the most pivotal portfolio to a returning mother was a deliberate step, because at that point in time, I had many women in my team who were married and who were planning to start a family. While I was not yet a mother, I felt that within the team by doing this elevation for a returning mother, I was setting a great example for other women to not feel worried about either procrastinating about their pregnancies or having even the slightest of insecurities that they would be short-changed upon returning.

'One of the other learnings for me from this experience was that a lot of times, we expect policies and organisations to step in culturally. That is absolutely the right thing to do, as it solves the problem structurally. But I realised that the biggest difference can be made by the decisions leaders take on a day-to-day basis. Leaders are not only acting as role models on behalf of the organisation, but they are also instrumental in creating more role models who inspire others and make them believe that "Wow! If it can happen to her, it can happen to me."'

Challenge the stereotype

'Many times, I have heard comments like "She won't like this profile, it's too hectic for her as it involves rigorous market travel" or "This is too unstructured a role for her to cope with" or "She is just back from her maternity leave, let us start her with a transition project which is easy to manage". This mindset can only change when we start offering these roles to women rather than assuming that they will not be interested in taking them up. I always propagate that as leaders, we need to trust our female talent with high-stakes projects—only then will women get prepared for leadership roles themselves. We have to be willing to stretch a woman as much as we are willing to stretch a man. Give her the confidence to take chances and be okay with both success and failure.

'Also, looking at this from a pure business standpoint, if over 70 per cent of consumer purchase decisions are made by women, it makes sense to promote a fair representation of women in the boardrooms and in senior roles across streams, from sales to marketing to operations, where they can contribute more directly to the decisions being made to serve their demographic.

'Thus, it is important that organisations challenge the stereotypes at all levels and bring in true diversity right to the boardroom of not only gender, but also of point of view, educational background and personalities. This will beyond a doubt flourish businesses.'

Big change through serious sponsorship programmes

'Organisations need to go beyond mentorship and career guidance and adopt sponsorship for talent. This will entail leaders and senior management to be invested in the success of their sponsees by helping them navigate the organisation both formally and informally, providing them visibility at important forums and access to good projects for career progression, and presenting a strong case for them during promotion discussions. Once more and more companies embrace true sponsorship, we will see massive progress towards gender inclusion.

'We often hear that remarkable leaders leave leaders behind. That is the kind of leadership all of us should aspire to abide by in some way or the other so that we leave behind people who are even better than us. An organised set-up of sponsorship can help achieve this. So sponsorship is definitely a practice that should travel across industries.

'The sponsors are the vocal force of good for employees at mid-management levels—a level where there is maximum attrition of women. This is also the time when most women find it increasingly difficult to network, given the disproportionate level of household and caregiving responsibilities on them. This is when sponsorship can really help by ensuring that a capable woman does not become out of mind just because she is out of sight. An invested sponsor is willing to take a stand for a capable candidate and will ensure that she gets exposure to growth projects suited to her capabilities and ambition. Thus, the adoption of sponsorship and the resulting behavioural change can solve the problem of the thinning funnel of female talent to a great extent.'

The importance of flexibility

'Since I have worked with teams which have predominantly women—between a newly married woman to an expectant woman to a returning mother and a mother with grown-up children—you can see that each woman is juggling multiple balls. This clearly shows that the pressure on women from a time capacity perspective is immense. One of the things I would say is a positive outcome of the COVID-19 situation is that the insecurities that most organisations had with respect to seeing employees in the office have now gone away. There is much greater empowerment of the individual and a much greater focus on results. This offers enormous flexibility to people to be able to be a part of the conversation despite physically not being part of the discussion within the room. Organisations should encourage more and more of this flexibility so that employees can thrive without being judged for their personal commitments. This will help both men and women.'

Organisations' role in maintaining the parallel track of personal and professional lives

'I realised during my stint in Paris how difficult it was for women to juggle work and families that they often chose to put off getting pregnant till much later in their lives. In my view, having a family and creating a home are all beautiful natural progressions in the life of a person. Hence, when an employee chooses to have a child, an organisation should be committed to making it easy for them to manage both their professional and personal commitments.

'It is a well-known fact that a woman's body clock is inversely proportional to her professional milestones. To take off this pressure, organisations can support their employees in exercising the choice of how and when they would want to have a child. For instance, today some companies have started covering the medical expenses for women who wish to freeze their eggs.

'This to an extent takes away the pressure of the ticking body clock and places the choice of when to embrace motherhood in the woman's hands. This I feel is a very pragmatic way for a woman to embrace choices. Personally speaking, my husband and I chose to have kids after 12 years of our marriage since we were both professionally driven and focused on our careers. This choice worked very well for me. As women, each of us has to make this choice and let me add here that these choices cannot be taught by a manual or a textbook, it comes with experience and a hunch for what works for you the best. With the advancements in medicine, fertility management is easier compared to what it was years ago. And organisations which are open to educating employees and providing insurance coverage for fertility management such as for freezing eggs, IVFs, etc., go a long way in making the workplace a level playing field for both men and women.'

Role of advertising as a gender equaliser

'Today organisations are realising that they can use their brands to propagate a change towards the right course of action in societies. For instance, there is a change towards showing men doing laundry, cleaning and cooking in some adverts. It's about changing the narrative towards making household work gender-neutral. And these changes are subtle, but they sure help in bringing about a shift. But I think in this journey only baby steps have been taken so far and there is space for all of us to do a lot more. That said, I am hugely optimistic that things will continue to improve.

'Let me share a market insight here—people in India get hugely influenced by popular celebrities. When you see celebrities like Virat Kohli and Anushka Sharma, you see two successful careers, both supporting each other as husband and wife and as new parents—this aspirational behaviour gets modelled by a lot of college kids, where they look for the same qualities in their life partner. By taking Virat's and Anushka's example, they believe that two successful people can come together and create shared success. The kids feel that when they choose their partner, none of them has to give up their career—they can embrace marriage and parenthood as true partners who support and stand up for each other. So I feel all these influencers have a huge role to play in equalising gender, be it advertisers or celebrities.'

The power of thriving dual careers

'My last two cents on making an equal corporate playfield for both men and women is encouraging dual careers. More and more couples navigating through their careers together and helping each other succeed is probably the best behaviour that can encourage more women to strive to succeed and pursue their passion. Only when more men experience the joys and challenges of being a working couple and raising a family together will they start relating more to the issues a female colleague faces. So, for gender equality to truly thrive, dual careers have to thrive.

'Organisations can help in this to a great extent. If a couple works for the same organisation, then both their careers should be managed sensitively. For instance, if the job requires international stints or rural postings, help the couple to be at the same station. This should be specially taken care of if they have children.

'Thus, organisations need to find ways to give a matching level of exposure to both the partners in the same country or city. This will help both of them to stay the course rather than one of them dropping off.'

13

The Conduct of Juniors

The only thing worse than training your employees and having them leave is not training them and having them stay.

—Henry Ford

Founder, Ford Motor Company

Amara is a VP in an investment bank. She is in her mid-30s. She is married and her husband works as a relationship manager in a wealth management firm. Amara has been with her current employer for almost 10 years now.

When Amara had her first child, both she and her husband were working in London. As a first-time mother, she decided to take a sabbatical for two years to focus on her pregnancy and spend invaluable time with her daughter during her childhood.

Luckily for her, when Amara decided to join back after her sabbatical, the company was running a campaign encouraging women on a career break towards a second career inning. Under the campaign, they were reaching out to female ex-employees who were keen to return to work full-time. Happy to know about this, Amara decided to explore the opportunity. During her discussions with the team, she highlighted her plans of relocating to India where she would be happy to join the firm's local office. Things moved forward swiftly and Amara was able to move back to India with her family.

The India office had a small team of 25 people; among them, 10 were senior management—MDs and directors, 5 were Amara's peers and 10 were at mid and junior levels like associates and analysts. She noticed that she was the only woman who was a VP in the India office, and there was only one woman who was an MD, while at mid and junior levels there were two girls. Thus, in an office of 25 people, there were only 4 women occupying front-office roles.

Amara also noted a few cultural changes in the operating style of the India team. During project allocations by the VPs, she noticed a preference given to male employees under the impression that boys could work more efficiently and for longer hours. Amara was facing similar challenges when it came to her interactions with some of the MDs, though the bias was more covert at such senior levels.

With time, Amara began to notice the difference in the behaviour of subordinates towards her as opposed to her male colleagues. Her junior colleagues were more inclined to argue when criticised by her but readily accepted feedback from senior male bosses. It was clear that they challenged her authority more frequently and with greater ease than that of the other team heads.

After three years with the India team, Amara found out that she was expecting her second child.

She continued with her existing projects and was open to taking new but less strenuous projects. She was upfront and practical about not taking very high-intensity work that involved long hours so that she could do justice to them while being stress-free. But, she soon noticed that the junior staff on her projects would constantly undermine her and try to weasel out of her projects since she would be on maternity leave soon and not be around during the appraisals. While she was always viewed as less capable than her male counterparts, Amara's pregnancy was seen as a further stumbling block in her career by her junior colleagues.

Amara was shocked to see young fresh talent holding such regressive views. She got thinking about whose failure this was, the organisation's and its management's in particular or society's and its upbringing at large?

This is not Amara's story alone. Many women at senior positions face the 'female boss' bias. These biases stem from years of social conditioning that associates men with leadership positions and women with emotional, subservient ones. These biases lead to a difference in behaviour towards male and female bosses. Subordinates often look down on feedback from female bosses, while male managers find it easier to demand accountability from their teams. This lack of belief in women's leadership capabilities also prompts subordinates to subvert women in senior roles, when clearly they would not dare to behave similarly with male managers.

Let us now go through the solution themes that can go a long way in building an inclusive culture where all employees can thrive across all levels:

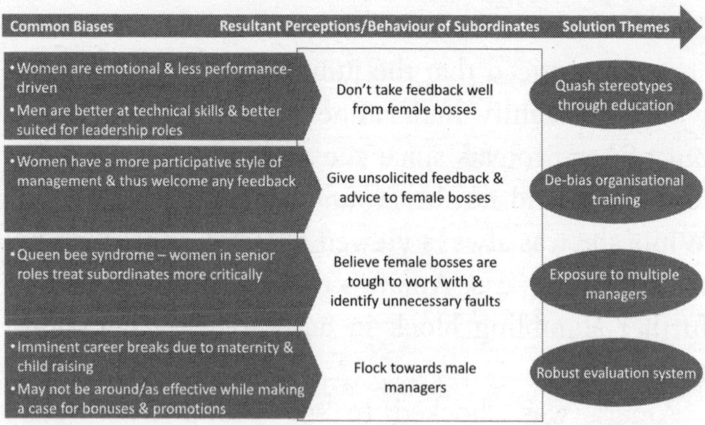

Education

Education is not the learning of facts, but the training of the mind to think.

—Albert Einstein

Theoretical physicist, Nobel Prize in Physics 1921

The first crucial step towards achieving inclusivity and getting respect from juniors at the workplace is to give them an inclusive education right from the beginning. Introduce it in schools as part of children's curriculum. They should learn that merit, and not gender, is the yardstick to determine one's capabilities, resulting in the opportunities they can grow into. This has to be supported by the behaviour of parents at home, where they treat their children equally. Paving the way forward, Schneider Electric India, under its initiative 'Jagriti' has designed a school curriculum targeted at teaching children about gender stereotypes.[1] The aim is to shape the right attitude in children from a young age.

The lessons on inclusion and gender equality need to be sustained throughout a child's education, through junior school, high school, college and beyond. Sadly, even today in MBA colleges—where the gender ratio is quite skewed and a handful of girls are competing with a far greater number of boys—signs of prejudiced behaviour can be seen. Gender ends up taking the front stage, shadowing the hard work and achievements of many young girls. People forget that these girls successfully competed with the boys to reach where they are. During the summer internship season and at the final placements, it is common to hear comments like 'She got through the interview because she is a girl.'

'She has dressed well for the interview; looks like she will woo her way into the company.'

'She was selected over me because of her looks; she does not stand a chance intellectually.'

This gendered approach should be corrected at its inception by educating the younger generation about stereotypes and biases right from the primary school level. Lessons in equality need to form a part of the formal curriculum for children.

Once a sensitised crop of young adults joins the corporate workforce, we will see a clear shift in

[1] https://infra.schneider-electric.co.in/supervision/images/annualreport/annualreportcef6OBz0m3.pdf

functioning within organisations. There will be more balanced teams, and it will reflect in work output too. When an organisation has more diverse teams where women are not just submissive placeholders but are active participants, better results are obtained. Then instances like Amara's can finally be uprooted.

If there's one drive that needs to be as famous as the Marine Drive, it is the De-bias Drive

It is important for organisations to continue with gender equality sensitisation and dialogue through corporate L&D programmes. These trainings need to be a part of the induction process of every employee who is hired in the organisation, irrespective of the position they join at. The de-bias drive has to continue through interventions in the form of formal training, informal sessions, role play, quizzes, etc., to be conducted at regular intervals. Many organisations do such events every quarter.

Planned exposure to juniors

The only source of knowledge is experience.
—Albert Einstein
Theoretical physicist, Nobel Prize in Physics 1921

It is important for junior employees in an organisation to gain diversified experience by working with multiple seniors and by getting exposure to a variety of projects.

Only when they work with different managers, both men and women, and get to handle both strategic and operational projects will they get to hone their interpersonal skills and eventually become well-rounded professionals. This also ensures that people don't get stuck in their comfort zone and can challenge any biases they may be holding on to. The queen bee syndrome often leads subordinates to think of female bosses as unfairly critical, especially of women. When juniors get to interact with a diverse set of seniors for professional guidance and get to hear their experiences and learnings, it moulds them to be more open-minded. With position comes authority, and everyone has their own style of exerting the same. There is limited point in generalising observations about any gender.

Robust performance evaluation systems

To be effective and yield results for your business, performance management must be a year-round process with no end.

—Teala Wilson

Talent management consultant

The importance of an objective evaluation system cannot be stressed enough. An organisation that gets this right sets itself on the road of superior financial performance, high brand value and a thriving merit-driven culture for all its employees. A well-defined evaluation system gives each employee confidence that their performance will be fairly appraised free of any manager bias. This approach motivates junior employees to be rightly focused on their work rather than getting involved in any sort of office politics. This also limits the probability of juniors getting affected by the sabbatical of any of their managers, be it for maternity or otherwise, since they will have the confidence that their performance is being routinely evaluated and recorded in the evaluation system. Supported by the regular manager feedback sessions based on the pre-defined key responsibility areas (KRAs) and KPIs, this will also help the junior staff to recalibrate and work on any improvement areas. It also leads to clarity on matters of promotion and variable pay and establishes performance as the only yardstick for progressing in the organisation.

To further support these solutions, adopting a data-driven approach to track the effectiveness of these policies will ensure that gender inclusion is actually being practised and is not just limited to paper. Since numbers don't lie, put analytics to good use:

- Take a random set of people from the junior pool and study how projects are being distributed among them—is everybody getting a good mix of strategic and operational projects?
- Are reporting managers working with a good mix of people or are they sticking to their comfort zone of a few people?
- Collect employee feedback on the quality of their mentoring experience.

These concerted steps will bring a change in the mindset of juniors towards equality and build an overall healthy organisational culture.

#RainmakerSpeak

Reeba Chacko, partner (head corporate), Cyril Amarchand Mangaldas

Law is one of the professions that attract considerable female talent. Law colleges can boast of an almost equal gender ratio at enrolment. But with career progression, the proportion of women drops. The average percentage of women making up the partnership at 30 top Indian law firms, for which data was available, stood at 30 per cent in 2018–2019.[2]

So naturally, when I got the opportunity to interact with Reeba Chacko, I jumped at the chance to get some insights.

Reeba Chacko is a partner and head of corporate practice at CAM. She has extensive experience of over 20 years in stringing together complex private equity deals, mergers and acquisitions (M&A), joint ventures and VC (venture capital) investments. She has represented both foreign and Indian clients with great ease and finesse across multiple complex situations. She is the national head of CAM's general corporate practice, overseeing over 350 lawyers including over 60 partners across 6 offices.

Reeba has numerous awards to her credit—she was ranked in Band 1 for M&A and Corporate and Band 2 for Private Equity by Chambers and Partners 2018–2021. She is also one of the 13 named lawyers from India in Who's Who Legal and was awarded the Economic Times 40 under Forty award in 2017.

[2] https://www.legallyindia.com/india-unleashed-editorial/women-in-indian-law-firms-in-a-growing-minority-20190601-11000

An unintended career path

Reeba grew up in an environment where her parents were focused on her education. Her father is a retired judicial officer. Reeba was a science student who was inclined towards pursuing biomedical engineering. She wrote the exam for the National Law School of India University (NLSIU), Bengaluru, to give company to a friend, and as fate would have it, she got through. Given how prestigious an admission into NLSIU is, Reeba decided to give it a go. The five years at NLSIU moulded her to love law, and she decided to pursue it as a career and joined the firm then called Amarchand Mangaldas.

Though Reeba's story is different as she happened upon the field of law by chance, I nonetheless asked her what attracts so many women to law and why the numbers reduce as one moves up towards partnership level.

Reeba presented a very practical perspective here, 'Over the course of last several years, the legal profession in any form has become even more attractive and interesting to many young aspirant professionals as it is being treated as a qualification that now opens up a very wide and varied variety of opportunities in one's career, from court practice (which earlier was considered the only form of legal practice) to corporate practice to teaching to not-for-profit initiatives to the judiciary and many others, each one very exciting in its own unique way. Earlier, I remember parents considered the legal field as precarious for women because of some of the stereotypes attached to it. That has changed and is mostly long gone. Speaking of the world of transactional practice I come from, in the 1990s or so, corporate practice became a very large part of the legal world and continues to be a thriving vertical today with the opportunities it provides. And with opportunities available that seemed to be more gender-neutral to a large extent as compared to some other professional fields, women found this a great career option as well.'

My next question was, why do women drop off the pipeline and how can we stop it? 'Girls, after the initial years of practice, whether in their late 20s or 30s, moving into their next phase of life—of starting a family, becoming mothers, some having to take care of parents or other dependents—find themselves in a difficult situation in trying to balance their professional and personal lives. And this has been a big reason for drop out after the first few years of joining the profession. The solution is twofold: first, women need to make a strong support system around them to help them, especially in the initial years to find a fair balance between work and personal life—support of your family and other infrastructure is important to be able to strike a successful balance; second, a supportive stance by the organisation. For instance, for women returning from maternity leave, organisations can offer a flexible work environment, allow them to start with a partial working day perhaps for the first few weeks when they return, then gradually increase it as they settle down better. This helps them settle in the office, form a new routine for themselves and gradually find a new balance between work and personal life. Some organisations like ours are offering dynamic work policies that may even include the opportunity to "work from any way" or "work from home" to suit your needs while not compromising work in any way. Just imagine how much this can help new mothers, employees (both men and women) with dependent parents or young kids.'

The power of networking

The most commonly mentioned stumbling block for a woman's professional life is limited networking. The concept of networking has been set up in a way that it favours men more than women. While it's easier for men to wine and dine with clients and colleagues, women always carry extra baggage on how they may be perceived when asking clients or colleagues out for drinks. I asked Reeba how she approaches networking.

'I am not sure I agree that networking as you call it is "a stumbling block". Let me tell you what has worked for me over the years. First of all, I take the responsibility for my own safety and personal comfort very seriously. And I don't go beyond my comfort zone in some aspects. I choose only such forms of networking that I am comfortable with, especially when outside the office. Whatever suits my intrinsic nature as a person. For example, there may be a time that a one-on-one dinner meeting at a suggested place does not work but you prefer a lunch meeting at another place of your choice. And if so, I would unhesitatingly suggest lunch or coffee or one-on-one office meetings because that is what is suitable for me in some situations. If because of this you lose a client or a matter (which I am not saying is likely to be the case), then I would be fine with it because it's a choice that I have made. I would not take it personally, and I definitely would not pressure myself to change on these aspects that would take me to a zone not comfortable for me. I believe that at the end of the day, the work would speak for itself... I would like to believe that I have not fallen behind in my career because I chose to take a stand on these matters or because of any choices I have made.'

Answer to biases

On similar lines, I asked Reeba about losing out on clients who may have some conscious or unconscious bias and would be more comfortable working with a male lawyer.

'The instances of such biases have reduced in my experience over the years, but that said, it could still exist at times. Say I come across a client who seems more comfortable interacting with a male colleague or is rather uncomfortable with a woman. This could of course affect me in the moment, but the feeling stays just for the moment. I would not stress myself to force the client to engage with me in the first instance but offer a face that they prefer and let the client see my value add on the job rather than right at that moment. I would instead channel my energy and attention to another client or project. So, I choose my battles rather than fretting over every such incident. I am fine to pass on such clients if I have to, but I make sure that their bias doesn't reflect on me as a professional and negatively affect me in any way. I tell myself "their loss" and move on. I think we should just let our work speak for ourselves. And it will speak.'

Role of influencers

We further moved ahead in our discussion to talk about the role of different influencers who have an impact on employees.

Talking about the role of managers, Reeba mentioned, 'We should not let a woman miss out on an opportunity because of her gender. Organisations must see to it that their managers evaluate their teams based on merit and merit alone, not gender or any other extraneous circumstances.

'Let me give an example here—if someone is expecting a baby, she is likely to take a maternity break in career in the short term, and she is due for a promotion. There are two ways to approach this: postpone the promotion till after the maternity leave, and say, "Let us revisit this in the next round once you decide on your way forward"; or consider her like any other candidate at present.

'Even just from an organisation's point of view, choosing the first approach would be taking a myopic view. The careers of its people and their potential to contribute has to be looked at as being a part of a long journey together, hence the organisation needs to take a longer-term view. And I am not even talking ten years—a happy and committed employee who feels recognised and valued can add much more value within a short two-to-three-year timeline as well (versus an unhappy one). Hence, I would choose the second approach, as there is nothing that could make more sense even to an organisation than just valuing merit, even if it is an investment phase, and retain good talent in the long term, which is a great morale boost to its people and sets the right culture in an organisation. A culture where the managers focus on the merit and performance of the employee as opposed to considering any other factor, including gender, during evaluations of its people. Organisations are training their managers to learn to evaluate people right, including making them aware of even any unconscious biases they may be operating with.'

I was further curious about the conduct of peers and juniors. I asked Reeba if she had personally experienced or observed instances of juniors questioning the ability of a female team member or managers in her area of expertise due to a gender bias.

This is what Reeba had to say, 'Personally, I haven't faced such a situation. But it doesn't mean that these things don't happen at places of work. I can recall an incident I heard of where a few female managers highlighted the behaviour of a particular male junior colleague as being less respectful towards them (like not taking the feedback given seriously, being unresponsive) compared to how he would behave with male managers. In such instances, my stand would be clear—assertively and clearly call out such behaviour. There should be zero tolerance if your domain knowledge or your authority is questioned for the wrong reasons such as gender. The organisation should take a strict stand if such instances are seen and such behaviour should not be tolerated at any cost. To avoid such conduct from peers and juniors in the first place, appropriate behavioural training needs to be put in place to ensure that the overall culture of the organisation is that of mutual respect. And to give the message that any contrary behaviour will not be tolerated at any level.'

14

Guiding from the Front—Strategic HR

You cannot mandate productivity, you must provide the tools to let people become their best.

—Steve Jobs
American business figure, co-founder, Apple Inc.

In any organisation, the HR team plays a very important role in setting the right tone for gender diversity and inclusion. A CHRO is akin to a neutral umpire of a cricket match—they ensure fair play, no bias and adherence to rules, and maintain the spirit of the game for all.

During my conversation with Payal Gupta, she highlighted the pivotal role of the HR team in enabling any behavioural change in an organisation and stressed that a strong HR department is a prerequisite to effecting cultural change towards diversity and inclusion. They need to build their credibility by involving business heads and leaders in taking an active part in forming the diversity-and-inclusion strategy and in acting on it with accountability. Often the HR team gives in to the requests and demands of the leadership team when they cite paucity of time and/or monetary support for some HR initiatives. This is where the HR needs to realise that they are representing the interests of the organisation and not just the CEO. If a policy change or training or an initiative is time-sensitive and essential for the betterment of the organisation, then the HR must make a strong case for it and seek time commitment from the leadership team, too, to attend such sessions.

I have always been a proponent of the HR department being a mix of a supply and demand office. It is, on the one hand, the supplier of operational support to businesses in matters of recruitment, payroll, salary and incentive structure, evaluations and appraisals, and on the other, it has to play the strategic role of a demand office, as part of which it has the authority of demanding from businesses commitment and performance in matters such as diversity, inclusion, L&D initiatives, branding of the business in the eyes of employees, and culture of the organisation.

Let us here focus on the strategic role of HR in maintaining gender diversity and inclusion in an organisation. I have identified six crucial stages where HR can play the role of a neutral umpire in ensuring a bias-free culture where all employees can thrive based on merit and performance, and contribute towards building a strong organisation that performs to its best on both financial and non-financial parameters.

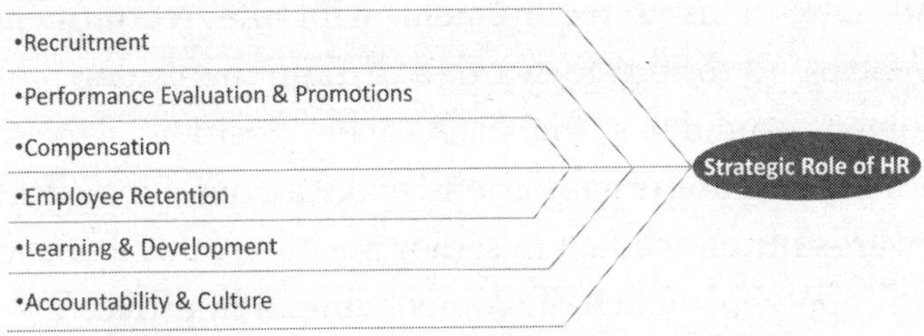

Recruitment

HR should be every company's 'killer app'. What could possibly be more important than who gets hired?

—Jack Welch

American business executive, retired chairman and CEO, General Electric

We have established so far that it is easier to maintain gender balance for entry-level positions but the ratio keeps getting skewed as one moves up the management levels. This is where the HR team's involvement becomes necessary. For instance, when a business is scouting for front office revenue-generating roles, HoD profiles or C-suite positions, it is important to scan the market for eligible women candidates. Organisations are often presented by recruitment agencies with an abundance of male resumes, especially for senior roles. One reason for this is the plentiful supply of male candidates given that men outnumber women at senior positions. This is where the HR team can plug the gap by doing thorough checks of the market landscape to ensure that no appropriate woman candidate has been left out of consideration. As a starting point, companies can state it as a requirement with the recruitment agencies to bring forward a certain percentage of women candidates for each open position. Unless more and more organisations make a conscious effort towards hiring women in senior positions, this demand and supply mismatch of women will not improve.

Internal employee movement is another area that the HR department can actively pursue. It is important to present growth opportunities to existing employees so they get exposure to different profiles that match their capabilities and skills. This not only leads to better employee retention but also helps the organisation in having the best-suited person do the job. These internal movements also go a long way for women employees who get the flexibility to explore new profiles within the organisation and balance it with their personal commitments instead of taking a break.

Exploring alternate platforms for hiring women can also be helpful. There are many career sites in India exclusively for women candidates entering the job market and also for those women who are looking to return to employment after a sabbatical. The HR department can scout for talent on these sites too. This broadens the talent pool for the organisation to choose from.

Evaluation

So often the problem is in the system, not in the people. If you put good people in bad systems, you get bad results.

—Stephen Covey

American educator, author of *The 7 Habits of Highly Effective People*

Having an objective evaluation system is the key to success for any organisation. It ensures a motivated workforce with clarity regarding their targets and a trust in the system that their performance will be objectively evaluated and rewarded.

This is also where a strategic HR team can play an important role by overseeing the evaluation process for each line of business in the organisation. It is important to conduct round-table discussions with all managers on their evaluations of subordinates and ask for specific examples for their feedback to rule out any unconscious bias based on gender, age, marital status or motherhood.

To ensure objectivity in the evaluation system, it is imperative to have well-defined KRAs, and under them, specific and largely measurable KPIs for each job role within the organisation. The HR department, along with the CEO's office, needs to conduct an annual exercise with each HOB towards defining the KRAs and KPIs for every profile within their respective business. For instance, for investment banking MDs, one of the main KRAs will be the revenue generated for the sector they are responsible for. The KPI to measure this would be the specific revenue target, split into the type of deal: merger and acquisitions, equity capital market and debt capital market. Another KRA is to build a pipeline of deals for the coming years. The KPI for this can be defined using the funnel approach: have a target for the number of meetings in a quarter, a target for how many of these meetings lead to a signed mandate and how many signed mandates convert to closed deals. By following this process-driven approach, all employees are made aware at the start of the year about what goals they will be working towards and the expected level of performance for each of these goals. This makes the evaluation process fully performance driven and free of any bias.

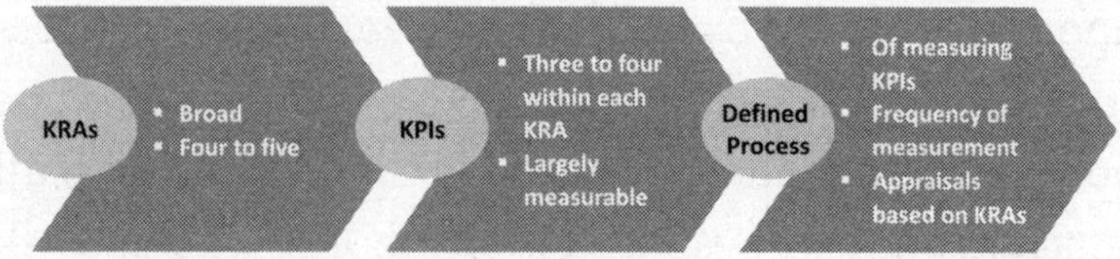

Promotion

The only waste of human resources is letting them go unused.

—Mark Victor Hansen

Motivational speaker and author

Half the battle is already won if the evaluation process is managed by the HR objectively, based on KRAs. When the talk of promotion comes and each HoD puts up their recommended list for promotion, the HR team must ensure that every eligible candidate is objectively evaluated for the promotion opportunity and no candidate is ruled out because of any bias at play in the manager's mind. For example, instances of performance-oriented assertive women being looked down on, on the pretext of being a bad team player, are not that uncommon, while the same behaviour is lauded in men. Thus, it is only the HR team that can assess each candidate with an objective lens and take a data-backed approach. They can do this by studying the personnel file of each eligible candidate, their qualifications, past work experience, ratings and feedback from the previous three evaluation cycles and prepare an independent opinion for promotion discussions with the respective managers.

Let me illustrate this point with a case study.

Aryan is a high-performing senior manager in a consulting firm. He has impressive billable hours and manages to crack two big clients for the firm that year. He is also a favourite of the MD given that he is a resourceful chap—good at networking, getting market intelligence on what the competition is doing, able to put together branding events, etc. Aryan, on his part, makes sure to maintain good visibility with the top management and behaves well around his seniors. He is always very humble around them and takes initiative to do various work streams, at times unrelated to his core profile. While Aryan is nice in front of the top management, he is quite rude to his junior colleagues and doesn't display good team spirit with his peers. A female consultant, Jenny, reached out to the HR department regarding his rude behaviour towards her, wherein he had rudely reprimanded her in the presence of several other colleagues for a trivial matter.

Jenny's complaint wasn't given much importance by the HR head and no action was taken against Aryan for his misconduct, barring a brief chat telling him how he should refrain from making undue remarks. No warning letter was issued, nothing went on his professional record, neither was he told the consequences if he repeated such behaviour. Such leniency towards Aryan was because he was indispensable to the MD, while his subordinates weren't. When it came to promotions, Aryan's name was recommended and strongly supported by the MD. The HR personnel failed to mention Aryan's poor interpersonal skills with juniors and peers to the broader top management. Aryan was promoted to the VP level without any opposition.

This promotion had a very demoralising effect on the team. They saw the organisation as one that supports and rewards reprehensible conduct, sexist, classist and rude behaviour. Most employees concluded that the leadership team had no interest in building a friendly and fair culture and was only focused on generating high revenue. That year saw very high attrition in the teams led by the MD and Aryan. A dent was formed in the company's culture and reputation.

To avoid such situations in a company, the HR team needs to display its authority in reprimanding unprofessional behaviour. In the above-mentioned instance, they should have put their foot down at the start by appropriately admonishing Aryan for his improper behaviour towards Jenny and even suspending him if the need arose.

For the MD who supported Aryan despite his behavioural flaws with his juniors and peers, the HR should have arranged behavioural training and recommended executive coaching on leadership and team building. Such assertive steps by the HR would have safeguarded the company's culture.

The HR team should not be limited to being a perfunctory department. It should be the central powerhouse of any organisation. Just like in a democracy, the judiciary keeps the government in line, similarly in an organisation, it is the HR team that needs to safeguard employees against unfair behaviour by reasoning things out with the business leaders in times of conflict.

Compensation

Clients do not come first. Employees come first. If you take care of your employees, they will take care of the clients.
—Richard Branson
Business tycoon

While we may have made some strides in improving gender balance in the corporate world, we still have quite a distance to cover. This is evident from the pay gap that continues to exist between male and female employees. Women executive directors (ED) earned 45 per cent less than their male counterparts in the last fiscal year (FY 2019) as male CEOs and CXOs took home bigger salary increments. Salaries of women EDs remained near stagnant.[1]

On this matter, industry stalwart Harsh Goenka, chairman, RPG Enterprises, says, 'This needs to change. I always thought one does not pay salary based on gender. The pay disparity shows the mindset, and that needs to change. Companies need to have multidimensional approach in hiring, retention and development of women.'

[1] https://economictimes.indiatimes.com/news/company/corporate-trends/glass-ceiling-pay-gap-between-women-and-men-ceos-doubles/articleshow/74019922.cms

According to Kiran Mazumdar-Shaw, chairperson, Biocon, 'As you rise up the corporate ladder, particularly as one reaches the middle-management level, there is an unfavourable bias against women in promotion. There is a natural selection of more men because the people deciding are also mostly men. The pay parity problem starts at that stage.'[2]

An assertive stance by the HR can go a long way in erasing gender-based pay disparity from the organisation. It is the HR's role to propagate one golden rule to be followed without any exceptions while making all hiring decisions, which is this—price the job and not the job holder. Once the organisation starts following this rule, it will help swiftly close the pay gap. This rule will disallow any bias to play out and ensure fair pay for the job irrespective of who holds it—a man or a woman.

Retention

In order to build a rewarding employee experience, you need to understand what matters most to your people.

—Julie Bevacqua
President, Rise People Inc.

The HR can play a key role in retaining women in the organisation who would otherwise leave for personal reasons. When we talked about Arya's case earlier

[2] https://economictimes.indiatimes.com/news/company/corporate-trends/glass-ceiling-pay-gap-between-women-and-men-ceos-doubles/articleshow/74019922.cms

in the book (Chapter 9), if the people policies were implemented in spirit, Arya may not have left the organisation on learning about her pregnancy.

Let's look at another possible scenario.

Maya is a highly qualified MBA graduate who joins as an associate in the investment team of a mid-tier bank. She is good at her work, with strong technical skills and a great attitude towards learning. During the initial training phase, she turns out to be the fastest learner amongst her batch mates. Seeing her potential, she is staffed with the most profitable and thereby the busiest vertical of the team—TMT (Telecom, Media and Technology). In line with the team's way of working, all associates, including Maya, are staffed on multiple assignments at a time, both business development and live deals. Maya is good at turning around the work allocated to her. She needs minimum supervision and makes few mistakes in her work. As time passes, her only issue with the work is the long working hours. Most days she has to stay in the office till two in the morning. Her parents start expressing their concern about this. During one of the deals, fatigued by too much work and lack of sleep, Maya faints and has to take three weeks off to recuperate. On joining back, she hits work with the same gusto. However, this time she makes a change and leaves the office by 7 PM and finishes any remaining work from home. During her evaluation, her manager gives her a poor rating because of this. He acknowledges that the quality of her work has not deteriorated, but she has been less visible in the office compared to the other associates. He is even open to having her removed from his team. This is where the HR steps in and reasons that if the work is being delivered, then the employee cannot be penalised. Shaina, the HR head, makes it a point to discuss this rating with the broader group and highlights how such a mindset can lead to the loss of a very good and qualified employee. They normalise Maya's rating to reflect her actual performance and ensure that merit and actual performance remain the basis of all evaluations.

Meanwhile, Maya can sense the hostility of her peers and her manager towards her. She decides to leave the organisation. On discussing the same with Shaina, she is asked to wait for a day before her resignation is accepted. Shaina thinks it through carefully since she doesn't want to lose a good employee. The next day, Shaina recommends an internal group movement of Maya to the TMT research team, which is on the lookout for a capable associate. This role also suits Maya's requirement of better work hours, and she is pleased to move to a new team. Shaina is glad that her initiative retains a high-performing employee without her compromising on any front.

This is how strategic HR comes into play in managing such tricky situations, where multiple stakeholders have to be appeased while maintaining fair play. Quick thinking and initiative on the part of the HR team can go a long way in retaining employees by helping them achieve a balance between personal and professional commitments. This also establishes the credibility of the HR team as a sounding board for businesses in times of conflict and as a lighthouse for career guidance for employees at large. Overall, it benefits the organisation by building a strong and loyal long-term workforce.

Learning and development

I absolutely believe that people, unless coached, never reach their maximum capabilities.

—Bob Nardelli
American businessman

Developing relevant L&D programmes has become very important in today's age. Keeping employees up to date with the latest developments in their respective domains contributes to a better quality of work and keeps employee morale high when they see that the organisation is committed to upskilling them.

Each organisation can either define this as a KRA for the CHRO or they can have an L&D head who works closely with the CHRO. L&D needs to be approached with a process that can be easily documented and followed every year:

- The L&D head, at the start of each financial year, should discuss with each business head the training requirement for their respective business. The L&D team should ensure that every role in each team is covered by the business head in laying out the requirement from the role and the kind of skill enhancement the employees occupying that role needs.

- The training calendar for each role should be holistic, including technical and job-related training, enhancing soft skills such as written and oral communication, and confidence-building exercises. For all managerial positions, training on how to give employee feedback and how to be a better mentor should be included in addition to the regular de-bias training for all employees.
- To ensure that L&D runs effectively in the company, the HR team should prepare a budget for it at the start of the year itself. The L&D budget of each business should be made a part of their respective financial budget rather than sitting centrally with the group office. This attaches accountability to the business heads towards the L&D agenda, which will cascade down to all the team members, ensuring that all training programmes are completed with seriousness and commitment.

For any organisation to succeed, it has become imperative for the leadership team to realise that L&D today is not only relevant for junior and mid-level management, but it is, in fact, even more crucial for the senior management and the leadership team, especially in this world of VUCA (volatility, uncertainty, complexity and ambiguity) that we are operating in today. For the top management, coaching in areas like decision making, risk-taking, negotiations, lateral thinking, stress management and general de-biasing is very important. Many companies go a step ahead and provide their leadership team and candidates in the leadership pipeline with life coaches who help them understand themselves as individuals first—their strengths, weaknesses and biases—and then work towards refining them as better individuals and professionals.

To further maximise the benefits from these programmes, it is very important that L&D as a metric is tracked by the HR division and progress on it is presented to the senior management and the leadership team. Any deviation should be highlighted and corrective action should be sought from the respective business head.

Accountability

Accountability is a key concept in moving an organization forward, especially in a challenging business climate.

—Cindy Tucker
Professor

Accountability towards diversity and inclusion is the only way forward to cover the gaping void between thoughtful policies and their true implementation. While the HR department remains the gatekeeper to ensure that diversity and inclusion as a principle is followed by each employee in the organisation, the accountability for ensuring diversity and inclusion in terms of hiring, leadership pipeline, mentorship and L&D lies with the head of each business. The HR department is there to guide and support the businesses in achieving these targets through policy support and strategic customised programmes on different aspects such as learning, upskilling, de-biasing and mentorship. In case a particular line of business or the entire organisation struggles with maintaining diversity and inclusion despite the support, then it becomes the responsibility of the HR to dig deeper into identifying the issues and suggesting specific solutions through industry research, peer practices, inputs from consultants, etc.

Culture

Treat your employees right so they won't use your internet to search for a new job.

—Mark Zuckerberg
Co-founder and CEO, Facebook

Culture, defined by the correct values and ethos, is what binds an organisation together. Though intangible, culture contributes greatly to tangible performance parameters such as the revenue of a company. If an organisation has a merit-led culture with objectivity at its centre, then employees remain motivated and perform to the best of their abilities, meeting and exceeding their revenue targets. This also helps enhance the brand value of an organisation, making it easier to attract and retain talent, and also helps connect with the customers.

As the management usually tends to lean towards and focus on the financials and revenue, it is up to the HR department to act as the custodian of the organisation's culture. We saw in Aryan's case how the MD supported him despite his unprofessional, culture-diluting behaviour. This was because Aryan was delivering on his revenue numbers. This gave a message to the employees that as long as business targets were met, they could treat anyone poorly. Such messaging by the senior management has the ability to deteriorate the organisation's brand equity in the long run and also restrict the talent pool for future hires.

Culture also plays an important role in defining the future growth prospects of an organisation. For instance, while evaluating a merger transaction, one of the key factors under consideration is the cultures of the involved organisations and how after the merger a coherent culture needs to be established for the new entity. The biggest deals can fail if this culture is not established right. The right culture is worth investing in the present to build a legacy for the future.

It is the HR department that can set the tone for the right organisational culture and play an important role in maintaining it. Any deviation from the values of the business has to be reprimanded with strict action. Revisiting Aryan's case—he should have been let go of by the firm on disciplinary grounds. When it comes to workplace ethics and conduct, no altercations should be tolerated and it is the HR team that can ensure this.

A strong HR department that is able to define and implement business-specific policies and attach performance accountability on diversity and inclusion to the HOBs is able to drive the organisation towards a merit-led gender-neutral success.

Now that we have covered all the influencers of the Power Punch framework, let us read through the full interaction I had with Payal Gupta. She explains the important role L&D can play in coaching different stakeholders of a company to ensure a gender-inclusive organisational culture.

What role does coaching and L&D play in influencing the behaviour of key corporate stakeholders—leaders, reporting managers, peers and juniors—to promote a gender-inclusive culture?

Organisations have now started investing significantly in L&D. Most of it is focused on spreading sensitisation and awareness on different topics, one of which is of course gender equality and inclusion. But in my view, this has limited impact in bringing about a change in people's demeanour unless it is supported by propagating the business case for having women as part of the organisation right up to the senior-most roles. So, more than just teaching about equality and de-biasing the organisation, it is important to have all the stakeholders, be it leaders, managers or middle to junior management, see the tangible value women add to an organisation in the form of improved financial performance, enhanced brand value, easy recruitment and more holistic decision making. For instance, one of our leading financial institution clients does this well. As part of their training, they show their employees how having a diverse workforce results in enhanced business performance and also improves their learning as professionals. This makes all employees respect diversity out of choice rather than as a compulsion.

In terms of specific coaching for different stakeholders, unconscious bias training is something which employees across levels should go through. This helps them realise if they are operating with a biased mindset covertly and how they can neutralise the same. Specifically, for the leadership and the managers, social norms awareness is very important. For instance, if there is only one woman in the meeting and she is asked to take notes, it sends the wrong message. Social norms awareness corrects this very instinctive behaviour, and all such interventions should at least be repeated quarterly to keep reinforcing equality and inclusion as an important corporate ethos.

If the leadership walks the talk on gender inclusion, it becomes easier to bring about a change at all levels in the organisation. Thus, sensitising the leadership is the most important thing to be done.

What should organisations do to ensure bias-free hiring, appraisals and promotion practices for women employees? What role can executive coaching and L&D play?

For bias-free hiring, appraisals and promotions, the first step is regular interventions of unconscious bias training for all the managers and decision-makers. Next, an organisation should be process-oriented and base all decisions on objective data rather than subjective inputs. For instance, for recruitments, companies must have a set question list for each role that evaluates a candidate on their competence to do the job rather than giving flexibility to employees to ask random questions related to the personal life of prospective candidates. As mentioned earlier, this process is called behavioural event interviews. Often female candidates are asked about their marriage and motherhood plans, while interviewers only focus on gauging men for their skills. Thus, women end up losing out on job opportunities even if they were most suited for the job qualification-wise. Having defined processes will rule out such biases. Follow a process-driven approach for evaluations and promotions too. Have defined KPIs for each role and objectively evaluate people on the set criteria. This way, employees also know what they are working towards, what are their targets and what is the level of performance they need to deliver to reach the next level. Another important thing to do is to have all managers undergo training on how to deliver proper performance evaluation to their subordinates.

Kindly share your thoughts on the role corporate policies and HR play towards effecting a 'true' behavioural change to promote gender inclusion?

The HR department plays a very pivotal role in enabling any behavioural change in the organisation. For this, the HR team needs to have a strong positioning within the organisation. They need to build their credibility to involve business heads and leaders to take an active part in all the requisite trainings and interventions. Often, the HR gives in to the requests and demands of the leadership team. This is where they need to realise that they are representing the organisation and not just the CEO of the company, and they need to influence and demand the same standards from the leadership team too. I ask for the same amount of time commitment and seriousness from the leadership when taking on any project with an organisation. I also clearly ask them about their willingness to receive detailed feedback on improvement areas. This is how

HR also needs to operate internally by exercising their authority for maintaining a fair and inclusive organisational culture.

Only when employees see that the leadership is also taking diversity seriously will it bring about a real change in the company, and policy implementation will become easier.

You have interacted with women leaders across industries. What, according to you, was the common trait in most of these women that helped them in achieving professional success?

Many of these women who reached heights of professional success did not give in to the masculine culture. They did not suppress their feminine side. They played to their strengths and were open to feedback to develop any complementary skills which they needed to better themselves. More importantly, they held their ground when they experienced or observed any bias and were not afraid to call out unfair behaviour.

There is a majority of men in the corporate system across levels (leadership, reporting managers, peers and juniors). How can they contribute to a gender-inclusive culture? Based on your interactions, do you see a willingness at their end to change things? Do they see any real benefits of gender inclusion?

There is a lot of cynicism even in some of the most educated people. That said, I see a ray of hope for even these men, since they too have daughters who would join the professional world one day. So that is a motivation for them to at least attempt to better things and move towards gender inclusion.

One important factor here is the willingness to do self-work, looking within. The larger systemic unconscious operates everywhere, so one needs to be aware of any covert biases playing out, and if one does take a wrong decision or observes unfair behaviour around them, it's imperative to stand up. This change needs to be visible both in personal and professional lives because people who are sexist in personal life will not be able to act as proponents of equality in professional life; they will operate with their set biases.

#RainmakerSpeak

Sonia Gupta, MD, Accenture

Some of the interactions I had added a lot to my perspective as an individual and how I see diversity and inclusion. One such enriching conversation I had was with Sonia Gupta, MD at Accenture based in Singapore. Sonia is a seasoned strategist with over 20 years of rich and diverse experience across industries and geographies. She works closely with the C-suite and boards of multiple companies spread across the Asia Pacific to help deliver their growth agenda through innovation. Sonia specialises in the field of strategy, innovation and leadership and development. She is part of the leadership team that looks at inclusion and diversity at Accenture and is very passionate about the subject. Her views on different aspects we spoke about reflected her depth of exposure and her practical experiences across organisations.

Trigger towards the diversity-and-inclusion agenda

While there is enough research on the benefits of diversity and inclusion, this agenda doesn't seem to be the top priority for many organisations. Given Sonia has solved problems around transformation and culture change for many organisations in her consulting assignments, has shared her experience with diversity and inclusion with other companies and been exposed to their own journeys, I asked her what triggers organisations to work towards diversity and inclusion.

This is what Sonia shared, 'Industries which need to reflect the society they solve for have a natural bent towards maintaining a diverse workforce and encouraging inclusion in their culture. For instance, you will see this in many consumer goods companies. Even in professional services, human capital is a big ingredient that drives a company's performance, so diversity in thought and consequently the workforce becomes of paramount importance here as well. Companies in these industries naturally gravitate towards diversity and inclusion across the board. On the other hand, there are some companies where diversity is not as naturally driven, but it is driven by their purpose, and they deliberately strive towards equality. To give an example here, a mining company or an oil and gas company that chooses to focus on diversity is not doing so because of the nature of its industry, but because its leadership understands the importance of diversity and the impact it has on their performance.

'Diversity and inclusion is now becoming important to both these archetypes and the key driving factor, in my view, is leadership. Many companies today are purpose-driven, have a strong link to people and have a strong diversity-and-inclusion mandate which is endorsed by their leadership team. Such companies want to earn profits with purpose. They make equality an integral part of their culture and every employee knows that it is a core part of their conduct and performance evaluation. Then, of course, there are policies in line with the diversity mandate, but unless the leadership takes it seriously the needle won't move much.'

Challenges along the way and how to solve them

It is often said planning is easy, implementation is difficult. Despite good intentions, and a push from leadership and policies, organisations often fail to achieve their inclusion objectives. I asked Sonia to shed some light on some of the key challenges organisations face and how to overcome them.

'There are two main challenges which come in the way: belief in the why of diversity and inclusion throughout the organisation through the use of language and data, and evaluating progress on it.

'The way to solve the former is getting the language right. I cannot stress enough how critical this is. One thing I always tell my colleagues and clients is "Equality is not the dilution of quality". This needs to be communicated well across the organisation—it basically means that all things being equal, pick the woman. This entails that the organisation is focused on building a high-performance culture with an incredible talent pool. Anyone who joins the organisation has earned their place. Performance discussions, hiring decisions and promotions are all merit-driven while consciously choosing the underrepresented demographic. Today, women are underrepresented, but if it were the men who were lacking in numbers, we would do the same for them. It is important everyone understands this in clear terms so that employees don't look at a deserving woman candidate as a diversity hire or someone who got preferential treatment.

'Diversity-and-inclusion initiatives, unless objectively evaluated, will miss the implementation mark. The way to solve this is by adopting a hardcore data-driven approach—there need to be well-defined targets on diversity. Everyone in the organisation should be clear on what they are chasing and they must be held accountable for it. For instance, x per cent women in leadership levels by 2025 would mean each business vertical should have x per cent women in the talent pipeline being mentored to take on senior roles. To ensure more commitment towards proper implementation, these targets have to be material enough and should be communicated to the company's investors and shareholders too. Many companies are unable to cascade down these targets to the entire organisation and then there are other organisations that are not ready to commit to these targets externally because they don't want to be penalised by the investor community and the shareholders if they don't meet them. Connecting targets, accountability, policy, the design of initiatives and continuously tracking the impact of execution on those targets is the key to moving the needle. These targets have to be used well to drive the required policy initiatives and ongoing management of diversity-and-inclusion agenda.'

The undeniable role of culture and an environment that promotes sharing

Further in our conversation, Sonia elaborated how important a role culture plays in ensuring inclusion and how an environment of sharing can help employees be on an equal footing in the workplace.

'Culture is a shared way of pursuing the organisation's key principles and passion. Diversity and inclusion needs to be a part of it. Let me give you an example. There may be a policy on flexible work hours, but if your manager prefers to see you in the office at late hours, you won't be able to avail the policy. It is not about the manager intentionally being difficult, but their reality is different from that of a woman who is running a house along with her career. Around 80 to 90 per cent of men in leadership positions have a spouse who doesn't work in an equally demanding career. Equally is an important word here—they may have a job, but it may not be as demanding. The wife, along with her career, is holding the fort at the house allowing the man to fulfil his professional ambition without any added burden. Such men, even with the best of intentions and being most empathetic, have no clue on what it takes to manage a demanding career and run a family along with its myriad of commitments like PTA, school events, kids getting sick, household staff unexpectedly taking off, etc. They don't understand because they don't face it themselves.

'The organisational culture has to promote open conversations on personal aspects without it reflecting on one's professional capabilities or accomplishments. It should be okay for a woman to not only say that "I can't make it to work" but to say that "I have a sick child who needs me" and a man should be able to do that too. There should be room for people to share and be their authentic selves. It is important to understand people better—you don't just need to help them troubleshoot for the moment but be thoughtful to systemically enable them to bring their best selves to work on all days.'

Getting it right—policy-wise

Sonia and I then proceeded to talk about the role policies can play in ensuring gender diversity and inclusion. We discussed that people have different personal journeys, and organisations may need to go beyond a one-size-fits-all approach. In that context, we discussed the parental caregiving journey of a woman.

'In India, there is support available when it comes to personal life, especially when raising children—there's help from parents or affordable childcare in the form of crèches and nannies. But it is enormously hard to manage because the quality of this support is inconsistent. There is a lot of firefighting.

'Because of the perception that this support system exists, organisations tend to absolve themselves from this aspect. There either are no policies to address the caregiving gap in Indian society (which relies more on women), or even if there are policies, people don't feel comfortable availing them for fear of being judged professionally. It is time for companies to break out of this model. It is about saying what is right to do for our employees today regardless of the support structure that each person has and how will we help them. This is where the crèche models at the workplace or close to the workplace come in.

'On policies, the organisation needs to be ahead of the curve. For instance, it's not about just maternity leave or even parental leave for men. Why not include leave options on fertility management like surrogacy, freezing eggs, IVF, etc.? In these situations, shouldn't we think differently about parenting, about childbearing? Shouldn't we change our policies to support the different needs of different people? My submission is that organisations should do so and have an adaptive modular fit towards certain policies, especially around leave and medical allowance, allowing employees the flexibility to utilise these as per their needs and personal choices.

'Further to this, parental leave and flexibility of parental leave in the first year are very important. Substituting maternity leave with parental leave is not enough. If you analyse the data, you will see that many men don't avail of it even when there are rules around how you can avail of it and, thus, the policy remains on paper. What's more important is flexibility in how you use the leave across the first year so that either parent can take time off as per their requirement.

'We could have policies for care for dependents, not just children and spouses, but elderly family members too. The definition of care needs to be widened. This could help us make a scaled impact for all employees.'

Advocating a life transition model to correct the thinning talent pipeline of women

Sonia had some interesting thoughts on how organisations can help when an employee is going through major changes in their personal life—motherhood of course being a key example where we see a lot of mid-management women dropping off.

'There needs to be a life transition model in place across organisations. Anytime an employee is going through a life transition (be it marriage, raising children, loss of a loved one, etc.), the organisation needs to provide policy support through paid leaves, flexi-work options and help with coaching. Different kinds of support could allow employees to navigate a life transition while living out their career dreams.

'For women at mid-management levels, support during the motherhood journey is important. Sometimes, peers/bosses (out of a protective instinct) tell pregnant women to take a step back from frontline P&L (profit and loss) bearing roles, do something "light" or take on a support role for some time. This is meant to be well-intended, and where the woman wants that choice for a certain period of time to balance her world, it's a good thing. However, two things are imperative to support women at this stage: this move out of a P&L role must be time-boxed and actively managed with a business frontline sponsor and coach who helps her transition back within a year or two. This coach is there to keep the woman leader connected to new opportunities, bolster her confidence as there is a tendency to have self-doubt once they have done a support role, and to actively position and manage a time-boxed transition, which is part of their success metric as a coach. For many women, a coach who helps them stay the course in their frontline P&L bearing role with additional resources might be a better answer rather than asking them to take on a support role in the first place. The thinning of the funnel can be stopped and reversed if this is proactively managed.

'Summing it up: intent, leadership, policies, culture, actions and objective evaluations—all play a key role in ensuring the success of diversity-and-inclusion initiatives. Multiple parts but all equally important. A culture of equality benefits all parties. As we stated in a research study by Accenture in 2018, "When she rises, we all rise".'

15

Inside-Out Wellness

Now that we have established the expectations from the employees of an organisation in ensuring a merit-led ecosystem, free of biases, let us focus on the organisational policies that can support these influencers in enabling this change. At the outset, it is important to note that these policies are for the overall wellness and development of all employees and should not be looked at as an extra cost to support a particular gender. These policies set the ground for an equitable and supportive organisational culture where people are not frowned upon for being different or for needing support for their biological needs. It integrates the employees and the organisation into a favourable situation, where the former group is able to see themselves as having a long-term career in an organisation that invests in them and is fair to them. These policies can be divided into two categories: hygiene and delight.

Hygiene policies are the ones that are basic yet essential in nature, some of them being mandated by law. They can be found in practice in many Indian organisations. Having these hygiene policies signals to the workforce that the organisation is cognizant of the basic welfare of its employees and is also taking steps towards creating a friendly work environment.

Delight policies go a step further towards ensuring employees' well-being and making them feel valued. These policies invest in the growth of employees as professionals and as individuals. Organisations that adopt more and more delight policies ensure a stronger Power Punch at play and are able to garner the most out of the talent they house.

The other way to look at these policies is to take the life-cycle approach. For every individual who is pursuing a corporate career, their personal and professional lives need to go hand in hand. Anyone who holds off one for the other ends up with the short end of the bargain. An organisation's support is the key to enabling employees to maintain a seamless running of their personal and professional lives. One category of support is ongoing in nature, covering health and wellness policies, compensation parity, employee networks, etc. The other is life-stage specific, such as maternity leave, menstrual leaves, career break, etc. It is a combined support of both hygiene and delight policies that an employee needs from their organisation throughout their careers.

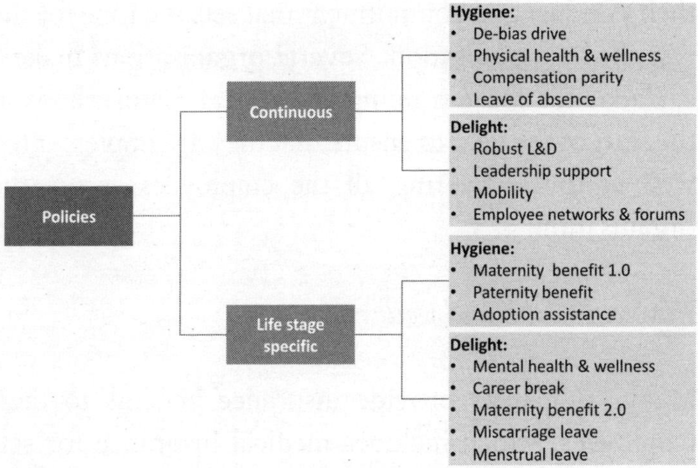

Hygiene policies

It is clear that any organisation invested in developing its workforce and getting the best out of them performance-wise has to create a healthy working environment. As part of this process, it is important to have the following ongoing initiatives at the base level:

De-bias drive

Biases play out both openly and subconsciously. Thus, it is important to keep the organisation ahead of the curve with training programmes and workshops for employees across levels. These interventions enable the employees to identify workplace biases and take steps to minimise the effect of such biases on their actions and decisions. These sessions are also important for the senior management and the leadership team since it is their conduct and commitment that sets the tone for the rest of the organisation. Several organisations make a calendar for these training sessions and workshops at the start of the year to ensure that they are implemented well in time, covering all the employees across the organisation.

Physical health and wellness

Many companies provide insurance benefits to their employees, which includes medical insurance for self and family and sometimes even for accidents and life. Additionally, there are some more valuable initiatives that an organisation can take for the continued physical well-being of its employees:

- Quarterly health check-up camps in the office
- Discounted comprehensive health check-up packages for employees and their families
- Office premises with a medical room with an on-call doctor for any emergency
- Gym facility or yoga area in the office premises, given that sitting has become the new-age smoking
- With ergonomic chair exercises gaining traction, educating and encouraging employees to do the same every few hours, such as neck movements, legs and arms stretching, and back exercises

Compensation parity

Maintaining compensation parity in the organisation is of utmost importance. Any two people at the same level of work, dispensing the same kind of responsibilities, need to be compensated the same. Of course, the variable component can be performance-driven, but the fixed salary needs to be determined fairly and be at the same price point for each level. Compensation for every role needs to be ascertained after analysing the following:

- Determine how the role is priced in the market by competitors and by larger organisations.
- Outline the profile of the person best suited for the role based on their qualification, years of experience and type of roles and organisations they've been through.
- Define your organisation's sweet spot for the CTC (cost to company) of the role, which would be an intersection of the organisation's paying capacity, the ideal candidate for the role and market rate for the profile. Also, take into consideration factors like employee policies, insurance benefits, medical, etc. At the end of the day, it is not just money that appeals to people; employee-friendly policies also go a long way in attracting the right talent.

Leave of absence

In addition to the annual leave policy that includes casual leave, sick leave and declared holidays covering major festivals, offer your employees further leave benefits to help them with their personal milestones, such as:

- Marriage leave
- Paternity leave

- Maternity leave for 26 weeks[1] (about six months)
- A day of special leave which an employee can choose to take on their birthday, anniversary, spouse's or children's birthday
- Bereavement leave, with no upper cap to help the employee cope with any major personal loss

The duration of the leave can be specific to each organisation and can therefore vary. Provisions for these leaves signal to the employees that their personal journey is also recognised by the organisation and that the leadership team is flexible and supportive in understanding their needs.

Now, let us direct our attention to the life-stage-specific hygiene policies.

Maternity benefit 1.0 <> Paternity benefit <> Adoption assistance

While maternity leave of 26 weeks is mandated by law (to remove the stigma of hiring women of a particular age and to discourage viewing women of child-bearing age as liabilities), it is important that the concept of paternity leave and adoption assistance be introduced in organisations. Providing paternity leave will take away the gendered approach we have towards raising a child to some extent. The few organisations that

[1] In 2017, the Maternity (Amendment) Bill was passed which increased the right to paid maternity leave for working women from 12 weeks to 26 weeks—the third highest in the world. The law is applicable to all companies employing at least 10 employees.

offer paternity leave observe that most men don't take it. Indeed, male employees should be encouraged by their managers to avail this leave to bring in the desired change.

Additionally, it is also important to extend support to employees who choose to adopt a child. Adoption comes with its own share of changes in one's life. For employees becoming parents via adoption, organisations should offer maternity and paternity leave and the associated benefits. Each organisation can have a tailor-made approach to these leaves. For instance, there can be a differential in the maternity leave:

- For women adopting a child under the age of one year, six months of paid maternity leave
- For women adopting a child above the age of one year, three months of paid maternity leave and an additional three months of unpaid leave with job certainty

For men too, paid paternity leave on adoption should be given.

There are some additional benefits that an organisation can offer employees who are new parents, such as:

- Flexible working hours in the first year of parenthood
- Paid or unpaid leave up to three months with no repercussions on career progression and continuity (the employee should be able to join back at the same position)
- Counselling on child care, work-life balance, parenting, etc.

Also, most importantly, more organisations should adhere to the rule of providing a crèche facility either on their premises or closer to the office to help employees of smaller children. This has been mandated by the Maternity Benefit (Amendment) Act, 2017, as per which establishments employing 50 or more employees need to provide a crèche facility, either separately or along with common facilities within a prescribed distance.[2]

Delight policies

Besides hygiene policies, the delight policies of an organisation play an essential role and should be given importance on an ongoing basis.

Robust L&D

An organisation's commitment to upskilling the workforce has gained quite a lot of importance in recent times. To ensure seamless implementation, have a budget earmarked for L&D initiatives and track it through the year, ensuring that the planned training sessions and workshops are delivered to employees. Bear in mind that L&D is not just for technical skills, it is also for improving other aspects such as soft skills, lateral thinking, conflict resolution, negotiation, etc. The aim of L&D is not just to make the workforce more efficient at what they do but to also enhance their personalities and make them smarter, more fair-minded

[2] https://pib.gov.in/Pressreleaseshare.aspx?PRID=1563830

and capable of taking on more than what they currently do. Only through regular L&D can they become well rounded and conduct themselves in impartial and equitable ways.

Leadership support

Leadership support is the key to having true gender equality in any organisation. Only when the top management drives it as an important agenda can the organisation make progress in that direction. It is an advantage if the senior management itself has equal representation of able men and women in their teams so that this culture cascades down as a KRA for the HOBs to build a diverse pipeline of employees in their respective verticals. Currently, corporate India has a dearth of women at mid and senior levels. But strong organisational policies implemented by the leadership's vocal support will surely improve the gender mix across all levels.

Mobility

Offer employees freedom of movement. It's time we realise that the idea of a nine-to-six job is passé. We are living and working in the era of hot-desking, and especially after the COVID-19 pandemic, more and more organisations should embrace it. As long as the work is getting done, the location of the employee shouldn't matter. Giving such freedom to employees instils in them a sense of accountability towards their work. Allow them a flexible work arrangement with options to work from home and flexible working hours—basically the freedom to get the work done in a way that they find most suitable, whether it is over emails, phone calls, video calls or in-person meetings. An organisation that is able to accomplish work virtually can grow much faster than one that believes in conducting long-drawn meetings.

Employee networks and forums

Form employee networks and forums within the organisation for people to connect and talk beyond work. This gives them the opportunity to learn from each other's experiences and connect with those outside their team. It instils a sense of belonging and connection with the wider organisation. This goes a long way for women in finding and connecting with other women in the organisation and in finding sponsors within the company who can guide them in navigating through the system and making fulfilling careers for themselves.

While the policies mentioned so far have been gender-neutral, meant to benefit both men and women, some of the life-stage specific delight policies are framed by acknowledging the biological differences between the genders. These policies come at no extra cost to the business. They are simply an acknowledgement by the organisation that the leadership team, together with the HR team, embrace diversity and are there to support employees through their personal needs. Just like organisations don't look down on policies for networking or health and wellness, they shouldn't disregard gender-specific support either, as the benefits of an inclusive workforce far outweighs the cost of any short-term support employees may need from time to time. Let us look at some of these policies in detail.

Mental health and wellness

In today's fast-paced world, mental health has gained paramount importance. For any employee, an ideal work–life balance is created when their organisation makes an effort to care for their mental well-being too. Employees should feel that they have a safe place within the organisation where their issues will be heard and addressed impartially, without giving any weightage to their rank. Several companies offer insurance coverage for therapy sessions. There is also a readiness in organisations for hiring the services of third-party professionals to help employees manage stress and confidentially discuss any issues they may be facing at work or with their teams. It may be useful for organisations to allocate an executive coach for a few weeks every year to the senior management too. This helps them discuss their dilemmas more freely and get a fresh perspective on pressing employee-related matters.

Career break policy

Allow employees time away from work with an option of coming back. Not only does this rejuvenate the employees but also builds a solid and loyal long-term employee base for the organisation. Employees can apply for a career break for reasons such as:

- To pursue higher education

- Paternity or maternity breaks
- Taking care of children/parents/spouse
- Medical emergency in the family
- Rejuvenation break to explore something different, such as writing a book, extensive travel, acquiring a new skill like scuba diving, photography, etc.

Giving this space to employees will contribute towards improving their productivity at work and in maintaining their mental well-being. One must remember that happy employees make a happy organisation, which translates to better numbers and thereby a happy set of stakeholders. Therefore, such policies not only make altruistic sense but also economic sense!

Maternity benefit 2.0

As part of maternity benefit 1.0, organisations offer paid maternity leave of 26 weeks, as mandated by the law. Some organisations with 50 or more employees also offer a crèche facility for the children of their employees, this is mandated as per law but the implementation is quite slow-paced.

As part of maternity 2.0, the organisation should focus on integrating mothers back into the workforce. Many women leave their corporate jobs because they feel alienated after they return to work from their maternity break. It is important to have an integration plan in place for every role, and seamless implementation of this plan should be included as a KPI for every manager.

Many organisations ensure that they stay in touch with their employees on maternity leave—these women continue to have access to office emails and get regular team updates. They are also invited to team calls and any virtual meetings. As they approach the end of their maternity leave, their managers regularly fill them in on what the team has been focusing on and which work streams they can get involved in once they are back. Once the women join back post-maternity, they are seamlessly integrated into their respective roles at a pace which they are most comfortable with. For the first two to three months after joining back, the HR team should touch base with them regularly to see that they are not stressed and check if they are facing any issues personally or professionally. These measures will help in plugging the leakage of women at mid-management levels and also help women in not losing out on crucial years of their careers.

Miscarriage leave

In March 2021, New Zealand passed the Bereavement Bill to allow parents to take time off after a miscarriage or stillbirth. The bereavement allowance allows employees three days of paid leave rather than using their sick leave. The development was much celebrated around the world with the hope that more countries would follow suit. After all, a miscarriage is not a sickness, it is a very personal loss and it needs time for both the physical recovery of the woman and the emotional recovery of both the spouses/partners.

But what came as an utmost surprise to me was that New Zealand is not the first nation to provide for miscarriage leave. India already has a provision under the Maternity Benefit (Amendment) Act, 1961, for a woman to avail paid leave of up to six weeks following her miscarriage. But not many women know of this provision, and there are fewer organisations that offer miscarriage leave to its fullest. Even if it is offered, women are passively signalled to not take more than a few days to two weeks of leave in such situations. This poor implementation is the main reason why despite being so policy progressive on this aspect, India does not get much credit.

Thus, to ensure holistic wellness of employees, miscarriage leave should be offered with full support to women who need it. Miscarriage is already a stigma in our society and it has both physical and mental implications for a woman. In such times, a supportive organisation can go a long way in helping the woman recover from this trauma. In addition to leave, the organisation should also encourage women to avail counselling if they feel the need for it. In many instances, women are not able to openly talk about miscarriage to family members. In such cases, an organisation that lends an environment of sharing and provides options of counselling can really help women navigate better such tough personal situations without being burdened by possible repercussions on their professional growth.

Menstrual leave

There are organisations in India that are now removing the taboo around menstruation by adopting a menstrual leave policy. This enables their employees to be open about a perfectly normal biological phenomenon, rather than hiding behind the garb of sick leave. This not only brings in a refreshing openness in the organisation's culture, but also encourages employees to not think of their gender as an inconvenience.

Happy employees are more productive employees. The combination of hygiene and delight policies goes a long way in engaging them and helping them unbundle their full potential. An employee with good work–life balance, who doesn't fear personal milestones like marriage and parenthood hindering their career, will perform at more efficient levels. This contributes to raising not only the happiness quotient, but also to the economic quotient with a spike in productivity.

Work–Life balance is about creating a life that flows with you rather than a life you have to power through.
—Jamie Marie Wilson
Entrepreneur

#PolicyOnPoint

Not long ago, the much-discussed menstrual leave policy was launched by Zomato, one of India's leading platforms for restaurant search and online food ordering and deliveries. The company announced 10 days of menstrual leave in a year. The announcement stirred a debate on numerous platforms, with many people in support of the policy and many others criticising paid menstrual leave, mainly on two grounds: additional cost for businesses and the underlying implication that women are a weaker gender, thus leading to potential discrimination at the workplace. I believe the spirit of the policy was interpreted wrongly and that these arguments have inherent flaws.

First, let's consider the argument of additional cost to the business. It should be noted that 10 days of paid leave out of 365 days is an insignificant amount. This cost can be easily justified if seen in the context of the benefits that a gender-inclusive workforce can bring to an organisation—maximised financial performance, better culture, larger talent pool and enhanced corporate brand, among other things.

There is enough research done on how gender-inclusive organisations perform better financially. For example, McKinsey's study 'Diversity wins' shows through its analysis how companies in the top quartile for gender diversity on executive teams were 25 per cent more likely to outperform on profitability (up from 21 per cent in 2017).[3] In fact, the substantial performance differential between the most and least gender-diverse companies can be as high as 48 per cent.[4] Unless we support women through their working lifecycle, which includes support during menstruation and maternity, how will they ever reach senior positions and leadership roles?

On the second argument regarding women being projected as the weaker gender, anatomically, men and women are different and there is no harm in accepting these differences. Women have added biological

[3] 'Diversity wins: How inclusion matters', May 2020, McKinsey & Company, www.mckinsey.com; Copyright (c) 2021 McKinsey & Company. All rights reserved. Reprinted by permission.

[4] Ibid.

needs when it comes to menstruation and maternity. To accommodate the same, they may need extra time off compared to men. Good organisations realise this and want to make the work environment better for all their employees. Any attrition due to a disregard of biological differences could hamper productivity at the workplace. I would argue that the tangible benefits of a happier and more diverse workforce far outweigh the notional costs of a few additional leaves.

Organisations promote a better working environment with multiple initiatives, for example, mobility benefits and flexible work arrangements. Naysayers do question these initiatives, citing a loss of productivity, but the broader cultural benefits of such initiatives go a long way in ensuring a highly motivated workforce. Motivated professionals understand what's important and ensure critical work doesn't suffer due to leaves they take, period leaves or otherwise. They display higher energy and are ready to take on additional responsibilities (including long hours and working weekends, if required).

While the intention behind menstrual leave is laudable, it is equally important to ensure its proper implementation. As with other gender-agnostic practices such as hiring, appraisals and promotions, the accountability of implementation of this policy lies with the organisation and not with the menstruating person. There is a need for workforce education to ensure the policy is interpreted in the right spirit by both men and women. There should be checks in place that ensure women are not discriminated against for utilising period leaves. Women also need to be educated about their options in case of wrongful termination or unfair appraisals. The solution to avoiding discrimination is not silence or quiet acceptance of the existing biased culture. Instead, any instance of discrimination needs to be assertively called out and resolved.

At present, it may be an uphill battle for companies to ensure the spirit of the policy is executed in practice, but the effort will be worthwhile in the long run towards normalising menstruation and creating bias-free working cultures.

Section III

CLOSING WORD: A NEW BEGINNING

16

Closing Thoughts

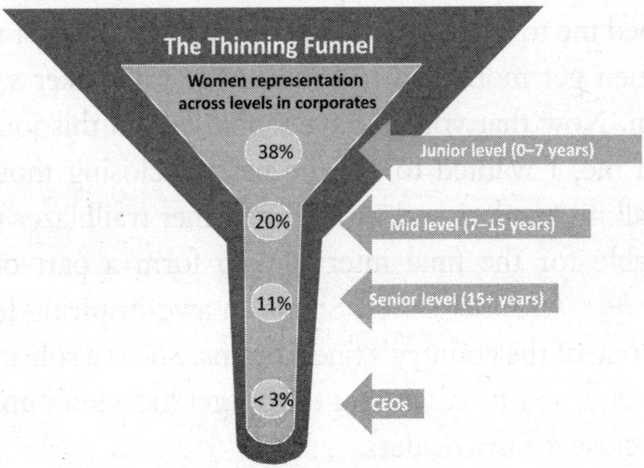

[1]

Everyone knows of the existence of this funnel and the disappointing truth that it is not going away anytime soon. I too witnessed a lack of women leaders in different arenas: corporates, academia, bureaucracy, etc. The paucity of female rainmakers always troubled me—could I ever become one? This question especially bothered me during my first pregnancy. That's when I decided to

[1] Women participation levels: https://www.livemint.com/news/india/women-s-representation-in-indian-companies-rises-11576086142768.html (study by management consulting firm Zinnov, in collaboration with Intel India); Women as CEOs: 'Women in Management'. Catalyst, 11 August 2020. Available at: https://www.catalyst.org/research/women-in-management/

unravel the mystery of the missing women rainmakers and started thinking about possible solutions. Driven by my passion for inclusion, I started work on this book with a vision of forming an equality handbook for daily life and the workplace. The multitude of interactions that I had with all the phenomenal women from different fields and who were at different points in the walk of their lives helped me to stitch together practical hacks so that more women get motivated to awaken the rainmaker within them. Now that you all have embarked on this journey with me, I wanted to get the best of closing thoughts for all my readers and I found no other trailblazer more suitable for the final interview to form a part of the *#RainmakerSpeak* series. She is an awe-inspiring leader and one of the country's finest brains. She is a role model to many, and it was an honour to get her views upfront and close for my readers.

#RainmakerSpeak

Zia Mody, corporate lawyer and founding partner, AZB & Partners

[She's] much more than just a lawyer... She has the ability to distil a business issue and offer an integrated global, social, and sustainable view. And she's blunt about it.[2]

—Mukesh Ambani

Chairman, MD and the largest shareholder of Reliance Industries Ltd, a Fortune Global 500 company and India's most valuable company by market value

[2] https://www.fortuneindia.com/mpw/zia-mody?year=2019

An iconic woman who is the founding partner of one of India's leading law firms, AZB & Partners, Zia Mody is a powerful force to reckon with. Considered an authority on corporate law, M&A, securities law, private equity and project finance, she has advised clients across the globe on marquee deals, such as the Tata Steel acquisition of Singapore-based NatSteel for close to US$500 million; the Tata buyout of Jaguar Land Rover for US$2.3 billion; Cairn and Vedanta; East India Hotels and Reliance, and UTV and Disney. IFLR1000 cited her as, 'an obvious choice for clients involved in large international M&A transactions'[3].

Zia's expert capabilities are recognised globally, as reflected in her appointment as the deputy chairman and a non-executive director of the HSBC Asia Pacific Board, VP and member of the London Court of International Arbitration (2009–2013) and a member of the World Bank Administrative Tribunal (2008–2013). She continues to serve on several government committees on financial reforms and corporate reforms.[4]

Zia is a role model for women in business in India. She has been listed in the top 10 by *Fortune India* in its 'India's 50 Most Powerful Women in Business' list for a decade now. In 2018 and 2019, she occupied the top spot on the list and in 2020, she has been listed as the second most powerful woman in business in India. Zia has been recognised as a thought leader across multiple forums, including *Euromoney* (Lifetime Achievement Award at Asia Women in Business Law

[3] https://www.azbpartners.com/our-founders/

[4] https://www.azbpartners.com/our-founders/

Awards), *Forbes* (among India's 10 most powerful women by *Forbes India* and *Forbes Asia's* top 50 power businesswomen), *Economic Times* (one of the country's most powerful CEOs and among top 15 most powerful women leaders), *Business Today* (among the 25 most powerful women), the *Legal 500 Asia Pacific* (leading individual for banking, finance, corporate and M&A and investment funds), India Business Leader Awards (outstanding business leader) and the list goes on...

Family providing the roots to stand tall and strong

Inspiration from Zia's father: A role model is the best teacher

Zia's inspiration to become a lawyer came from her father Soli Sorabjee, one of India's most distinguished jurists and former attorney-general (in 2002, he was honoured with the Padma Vibhushan for his defence of the freedom of expression and the protection of human rights).

Zia's father was a role model for her. She recalled how she would see her father working and conducting meetings and calls with his colleagues and she would always find this quite stimulating and challenging.

Learnings from Zia's mother: Strong mothers raise strong daughters

'I am the eldest of four children and was the only girl being raised with my three younger brothers. My mother,

Zena Soli Sorabjee, was a Baha'i by religion, which has gender equality as one of its ten commandments, and she took it very seriously. Hence, growing up I never felt unequal emotionally or intellectually. All four of us were encouraged by her to pursue our passions and work hard.

'My mother was pragmatic. She wouldn't prim her daughter towards domesticity. On the contrary, she always encouraged me to pursue higher studies, have a career and become financially independent.

'Fuelled by the equality in my parents' approach towards raising my brothers and me, gender was never an issue in my head while growing up. I was as confident as my brothers.'

Self-confidence: The greatest gift for a child

Zia said, 'My gender-neutral upbringing helped me develop an inner sense of confidence early on. The solid foundation of being brought up by a father who was proud of my achievements and a mother who was always pushing me to do well professionally set me up for professional success. My father jokes that I used to be a bully in my childhood days, but I take it as a sign of the self-confidence I generated during my formative years, which has continued to help me throughout my professional journey.'

Soli Sorabjee, Zia's father, said, 'She is headstrong and assertive. I observed this during her days as a barrister, too, that she cannot be bullied by anyone.'

If you are passionate, you will seize every opportunity and rise up against all odds

Talking about her early career, Zia said, 'Up until I completed my education in India, and then later in the UK, I didn't face any gender-related issues. Post that, I started my career working in the US. There too, I guess we were too young to face the proverbial glass ceiling. It was all a matter of performance, whosoever performed well, was brighter and was harder working got the better bonus. But when I came back to India to practise as a junior counsel in high court, I could sense the gender differences.'

Back in the 1980s, law in India was male-dominated, and Zia was among the two or three young female barristers while most lawyers and judges were men. That was when Zia felt, 'Oh my god, where are all the women!' But that was the reality and she had to deal with it.

Zia recalled, 'To start with, it was difficult to convince a typical hard-nosed businessman to trust a young woman. I could see it in many faces—why take a chance on her? I don't blame them, they were just not used to the idea of trusting a woman lawyer.

'Then the proverbial diffidence of any woman who worked back then was right in the middle of my world, and I had to work extra hard to ensure that I didn't make any mistakes. I felt that people were looking at me, I was like a strange animal to them. I was trying to fit in, I had to earn the trust of my clients and counterparts—I just couldn't afford to look stupid. This thought made my mental anxiety go up, and I developed a style of working per which I would read extensively, review every line, every page and every brief. If people would put in two hours, I was prepared to put in three. Hard work was my only mantra—there were no shortcuts. I knew that somewhere intellectually and emotionally, my clients would probably be more comfortable with a young man than a young woman, so I overcompensated at work (like a lot of women do at work). At times, it was exhausting.

'However, in a good way, this led me to micromanage every aspect of my career and to be abreast with every development that happens in my world. This has kept me in good stead professionally. I never took anything for granted—my education, my work, my cases and my clients.'

After the economic reforms in 1991, India opened its doors to foreign direct investment. Zia's friends and clients (from her US days) started referring clients who wanted to invest in India. Zia sensed an opportunity (plus it was difficult to manage being a counsel during the day and a corporate M&A lawyer at night given her working style). Around 1995, a small proprietorship called 'Chambers of Zia Mody' with a small group of 12 lawyers was born. This later morphed into AZB & Partners, one of India's top corporate law firms with a pan-Indian presence and 400+ lawyers.

Zia recalled, 'One interesting aspect was that because my clients came via recommendations from my foreign counterparts, I didn't face discrimination from foreign clients. They did not necessarily have the same bias which Indian clients had. In some ways, I was gender-neutral. The other interesting aspect was I could earn more if I charged dollar rates—I could hire better and on-board the best talent. It all made sense. For the first five to eight years, I catered exclusively to foreign clients.'

As years progressed, Zia earned a reputation for understanding the nuances of foreign exchange law, company law and being tactical at the negotiating table. Indian clients also started seeing the value she was providing to her foreign clients, biases were quashed and suddenly Zia became the go-to advisor for Indian clients too.

Over time, 'Zia, the expert' turned into 'Zia, the legend'. She has advised global and Indian powerhouses (including GE, Schneider Electric, Tata Group, Reliance Industries, Aditya Birla Group, Airtel, L&T and Vedanta Group) and leading private equity houses. Her clients see her as 'one of India's foremost corporate attorneys' who is a 'problem solver', 'meticulous', 'thorough', 'result oriented' and 'accessible'.[5]

Managing motherhood: Your circle of trust will take care

'My husband Jaydev and I have raised three daughters together. In line with Baha'i beliefs, we have raised our daughters to be confident individuals who can

[5] http://www.businessworld.in/article/Zia-Mody-A-Leading-Light/03-04-2020-188214/

achieve whatever they set their eyes on work hard towards it.

'In the journey of raising a family along with a demanding career, my husband played a pivotal role. I did not have a healthy work–life balance, but I have a wonderful husband who was always there for me and our kids. When I would be busy with litigation, Jaydev would work around his schedule and be more with the girls.

'My mother-in-law was also a great support throughout. I could work with a peaceful mind because I knew that my daughters were with the person who loved them a lot.

'This sense of comfort when it comes to one's kids is very important for all women so they can progress in their careers. A supportive family goes a long way to fix the leaky pipeline of women reaching to leadership positions.'

Zia as a leader: Clarity of thought is the key to effective leadership

'I think the leader's vision is important to drive this agenda. The tone is set from the top and that cascades throughout the organisation (if the tone is serious enough).

'Hiring is not much of a problem in our field. Law, unlike many other professions today, can boast of an equal intake of both genders at the entry-level. Thus, it is the leaky pipeline to the top which needs to be addressed by the leader with all seriousness. Here, you need a comprehensive multi-pronged approach and let me talk about some of the key levers which I have found effective.'

Setting objective targets and ensuring that they are met

'Let me share a conversation I had with a woman who was the MD of a male-dominated Anglo-American large mining firm. During one of her business visits, I asked her how she manages being a woman in such a business and how does she ensure the retention of women in her company? Her response was simple. She has assigned specific KRAs to all managers on the retention of women. If the managers don't meet their targets satisfactorily, they are objectively questioned about it. Given that their career progression (and in some cases bonus) is dependent on satisfactorily meeting their KRAs, they take their responsibility of retention of female talent seriously. Leaders should leverage this simple and effective tool to drive inclusion in their organisation.'

Objective evaluations and relevant nudges

'During evaluations, it is generally objective for us—deals worked on, clients retained and new clients added, among other things. Clear targets and KPIs help keep biases out of the picture. Sometimes, there are unconscious biases at play that are not in the favour of women, and relevant nudges can help.

'For example, if someone recommends a guy for promotion ahead of his female counterpart, I make sure to discuss the capabilities and performance of both members. Sometimes when you have a relative discussion, we find that both candidates are equally good and should be considered for promotion. It is just about the nudge to ensure there is a level playing field during evaluations and promotions.'

Operationalising a respectful culture among peers

'I remember when we were a younger organisation—many women went through the journey of motherhood. At times, some peers would look down on women colleagues who would have to take time off or opt for flexi-time for attending to the added responsibilities they had. My trick was to ease off 25–30 per cent of their work without making noise about it. Some peers would notice and create a noise. That's when I had a conversation with them to ensure they were being sensitive to the issue. I explained to them that we all have a long career ahead of us and smoothening this journey for all colleagues is our responsibility. At times, people did not agree with my views—I was clear that whether they like it or not, there was no room for grumbles affecting our work environment. There was no tolerance for that.

'As people grow in their careers, they empathise with this—mainly when they become fathers themselves. They want their wife to have a smooth motherhood. Men of today are invested in their daughter's education and career (especially in urban India). They take pride in their professional development and want their daughters to be supported by their organisations. I would ask this question to people if they would like their daughter to be questioned in her area of expertise based on her gender. And the answer is always a no! So, I ask them to be mindful of their women colleagues too, and it works.

'The idea is not to have an iron fist crashing every comment made against gender inclusion, but you have to explain to people that women are a very important part of the workforce and it makes a lot of financial sense to care for half the world's talent.'

The power of open conversations

'It is important to allow women to share their pain points and what they want. And these conversations have to be bespoke—it cannot be one size fits all. Each woman has her own kind of problems, for example, too much travel, nannies quitting all the time, a kid who falls sick often or no support infrastructure as the husband's job entails constant travel. The management and leadership have to be flexible here.

'What I found effective was to let women come up with their own solution. They know organisational constraints and what is doable. For instance, while we have six months' maternity leave, employees can discuss and choose part-time working or flexible hours, etc. We have created a small baby crèche on the ground floor of our office, and it is absolutely exquisite—employees can have their babies close to them and have the ability to check on them at any time. One of my female partners asked me if I could make her partner cabin next to a small cabin crèche for her baby and I did it with some ground rules and she managed. She was happy and so was I. If women feel that the organisation genuinely wants to keep them, then they stay back and add a lot of value.

'All of this has served AZB & Partners quite well, and the outcome is that about 37 per cent of our partners are women (sub-text is we have understood what makes them stay). We have retained as many as we can and continue to further our commitment to a better work environment.

'Advice for men—you spend as much time at work as you with your family. If you can be a good father, brother, husband, how hard it is to be a good boss or a colleague?

'Women in the corporate world have become very important, given a constant war for high-quality talent. More than the right thing to do, let's look at it economically too—you can't ignore half of the world's talent pool if you want the best. Once you hire women, you don't want to be investing time, money and effort on training them if you can't retain them.

'Since men today are the majority, they can contribute by being aware and sensitive to the needs of all employees in an organisation, including women. You may not have thought about it till now, but there has to be a first step in the right direction. Sometimes, encouragement from strong leaders and HR departments helps with that first step. Sometimes, you see the same challenges in your family and that's the moment of realisation.

'Male mentoring and camaraderie needs to be meaningful. We need a mutual opening up. It is a combination of the male boss/peer initiating a conversation when a woman may need flexibility, and women also need to ask for it. Organisations need to enable it through education, policies, specific targets and efforts from the leadership. The good thing is more and more men are aware and want to contribute; this makes me happy.'

Hoping for a more equal world for generations to come, Zia said, 'I would like to think women are in a more positive place in 2021! And hopefully, in the times to come, the world is more equal than it is today.'

I can comfortably say that by the end of my conversation with Zia, I believed that she is indeed the gold standard when it comes to embodying gender equality and inclusion both personally and professionally.

17

Call to Action

[Gender equality is] the great unfinished business of the 21st century.
—Hillary Clinton
Lawyer and politician

As a parent, be equal and fair. As an individual, be assertive. As a professional, be open-minded and pragmatic. As a leader, be free of bias and walk the talk on equality. That would be my earnest request to all my readers.

I'd like to reiterate a few key takeaways for different stages of life and where each one of us can make a difference.

A gender-neutral approach

History will judge us by the difference we make in the everyday lives of children.
—Nelson Mandela
Former President of South Africa

For grassroots change towards achieving gender equality in its true sense, the most important step is a gender-neutral upbringing. Only when we raise children by giving them equal opportunities and imparting the same set of values will we enable them to realise their potential. Therefore, the next time you come across a karate class, have both your son and daughter give it a try. Basic life skills such as cooking and self-defence should be taught to both boys and girls. Empower them to be the best version of whatever they seek to be; raise your kids as bundles of unlimited potential unrestricted by their gender. Don't let the conventions of society dictate to you how to raise your children. Bring in the change you want to see in the world.

My husband and I have taken a pledge to raise our child as an individual capable of realising her potential to the fullest by providing a nurturing environment for her to grow in. We won't let our parenting philosophy be governed by age-old conventions defined by gender. I invite all the mothers and fathers reading this book to take the same pledge and spread awareness around them (*#MothersPledgeToEquality* and *#FathersPledgeToEquality*). Let each child grow up freely to realise their personal calling unhindered by societal norms and definitions.

Assertiveness in action

Every time we liberate a woman, we liberate a man.

—Margaret Mead

Cultural anthropologist and writer

Just like we wholeheartedly teach our children 'A for apple', as adults let's wholeheartedly learn 'A for assertive' and see to it that we raise our voice if we experience any bias or observe any instance of it around us. United we will stand and win, while divided we will fall to the age-old inequalities and gendered approach to living. Let's walk towards gender equality with a consistent and committed effort with no deviations, because even one exception runs the risk of making it the norm.

Freedom of choice

May your choices reflect your hopes, not your fears.
—Nelson Mandela
Former President of South Africa

When it comes to the choices we need to make from time to time, just remember to do so with free will. Pave your own way as your circumstances allow rather than giving in to societal pressures and expectations.

While making a career choice, evaluate the organisation on the diversity management parameter and the nature of policies it has to ensure the inside-out wellness of all its employees. An organisation with a healthy representation of diverse people is not only fair in its practices but is also merit led, devoid of biases and performs better financially. Such an organisation can prove to be a better employer in the long run and be the place where one can make a career for life.

As I draw to the end of the book, I recall an African proverb, 'If you educate a man you educate an individual, but if you educate a woman, you educate a nation'. So, let's focus on educating all women, all mothers, and urge them to live up to their potential and pursue their passion rather than getting lost in the stereotypical template that society has defined for them. With a pragmatic, non-gendered approach to parenting, let the upcoming generation of girls blossom into empowered women and let the upcoming generation of boys turn into respectful men who, rather than feeling emasculated with the growing ambition of women, know how to share the load and live in a society of emancipated women reaching heights in personal as well as professional life.

While I pray, hope and work towards a new beginning, here is a closing thought for fellow parents:

There are two things we should give our children—one is roots and the other is wings.[1]

[1] Author unknown.

INDEX

ABOUT THE AUTHOR

Nishtha Anand is a strategy professional with experience in investment banking and strategy, and has worked across India and Singapore. She is a University of Delhi gold medallist and holds an MBA from the Indian Institute of Foreign Trade (IIFT), New Delhi. A seasoned professional with close to a decade of work experience, she has established herself as a collaborative young leader with the distinctive ability to ideate and implement transformation projects focused on people, processes and culture. Her interest in writing goes back to her college days when she was the editor of IIFT's finance magazine. She also has a white paper publication to her name on the topic 'Inverted Yield Curve and Stock Performance', published in the *Asia Pacific Business Review* in 2011.